Dedication

To Mark, my hero, whose faith and love are still felt; and to our daughters, Victoria and Alexandra, who continue to inspire every day. Their love, courage and determination are a true reflection of Mark. We were, and continue to be, four.

"There is a time for everything,
and a season for every activity under the heavens..."
Ecclesiastes 3:1

Contents

Acknowledgments

To commit to paper the most devastating time in one's life is incredibly challenging and could not have been achieved without Rachel Farmer, an army wife and dear friend, who knew the Hale family well. We served as wives together while our men were away. We shared good and not so good times. We shared laughter and tears, as this book brought to the surface both joy and pain that were not too deeply buried.

To Sir Jeffrey Donaldson, who has been a stalwart supporter since August 2009 and guided me along the path on which I now find myself.

To the Army Benevolent Fund The Soldiers' Charity, for their ongoing support. I am proud to be an ambassador for their work.

To my church, my minister Bobby Liddle for his sage advice, counsel, and strong faith, particularly while mine was battered and fragile.

To the Devonshire and Dorset Regiment and 2 RIFLES – our lifelong friendships have sustained me.

And finally in memory of all those we lost in Afghanistan and other theatres of conflict, recognizing the strength that is required by those left behind to go on alone.

Acknowledgments from Rachel Farmer

Brenda, Tori, and Alix Hale – thank you for allowing your story to be shared. Simon for inspiring me to write this book with Brenda. Our children, Tom, Georgie, and Will, for unstinting encouragement.

Tony Collins at Lion Hudson for supporting the book before it was finished, and Alison Hull for helping us through the stages to publication. Thank you to all Mark's friends and colleagues who have shared memories and given us insights into his life in the army.

Foreword

It is always a privilege to be invited to write the foreword to any book, but to be invited to write a foreword to *I Married a Soldier* by Brenda Hale and Rachel Farmer is not just a huge privilege, but also a deeply humbling experience. For forty years I was one of those "soldiers", and for thirty-two of those years my wife, Pippa, was the person who had "married a soldier" while I went in and out of Northern Ireland, Bosnia, Kosovo, Iraq, and Afghanistan. And we had a son who served two tours in Iraq and one in Afghanistan. So what do I know about the experiences of those left at home? Precious little, is the truthful answer. This then places me in the same position as the vast majority of people who will read this totally compelling book.

It has become something of a cliché for writers to describe the anguish of those left at home, dreading the knock on the door that would announce the awful news that a loved one has been killed or seriously wounded on operations. In generations past there was not even an officer on the doorstep but simply a telegram boy who passed over an envelope and cycled off. But it is the era of instant communications that on the one hand brings front-line news into the home, but on the other hand connects the anxious wife to the husband on patrol – and today, a kaleidoscope of husbands, wives, and partners are all part of that complicated but totally interrelated mix. Brenda Hale's anguish as Mark served Queen and Country on many front lines is as agonizing as it is authentic and tragic, but ultimately it is both pragmatic and conquering. For Brenda, Mark has never left her, but in her life after Mark's death in Afghanistan she has found strength in her family, her friends, her political work in Northern Ireland, and in her Christian faith. None of this will replace Mark – the love of her life – but all these things ultimately serve to provide purpose, focus, and hope for the future.

I Married a Soldier is a searingly honest account of one woman's life before and after the loss of her dearly loved husband on operations in Afghanistan. It is the integrity of her story that gives this book the authenticity which makes it so compelling. However, this book is not just a tale of sudden tragedy and its consequences; it is also an account of achievement against the odds, amid unforeseen and horrifically changed life circumstances. Furthermore, the structure of the book helps bring these changed events and expectations into perspective. Quoting from Ecclesiastes 3, Brenda notes: "There is a time for everything, and a season for every activity under the heavens…" All twenty-eight chapters reflect on a different time and emotion: "…a time to rest, …a time to dance, …a time to love, …a time to grieve".

Brenda Hale, inspired by her husband's memory and sustained by her Christian faith, has rebuilt her life in an extraordinary manner and is a profound example of someone who lives for others. Her work as an ambassador for the Army Benevolent Fund The Soldiers' Charity and her role as a Member of the Legislative Assembly at Stormont are just two illustrations of that life. For Brenda, the pain of the past and her hope for the future meet in her purposeful activity in the present. Of the effect of the loss of Mark on herself and her two daughters, Tori and Alix, she writes most poignantly:

> *It never gets easier, but I am pleased that his life and his faith are reflected in us, and it's on his example we based our lives. It may seem that we idolize him, and we do, but only as a*

gift from God. Knowing the outcome, I would do it all again, for not to have shared his life would have been much worse.

Like all those who loved him or served with him, I salute the memory of the late Captain Mark Hale, killed in Afghanistan on 13 August 2009, on operations with 2nd Battalion The Rifles. Moreover, I commend unreservedly this extraordinary account of Brenda Hale's most meaningful life after his tragic death – the widow left behind, who explains very simply, "I married a soldier."

Richard Dannatt
General the Lord Dannatt GCB CBE MC DL
Chief of the General Staff 2006–2009

CHAPTER 1

July 2009

... a time to rest

A lone red poppy wavered in the wind on the scorched plain. Crouched low in a shallow trench, a hunched figure was barely visible. His binoculars trained on a line of scrubby green bushes marking the banks of a brown stream, the soldier shifted his weight and sniffed. Drawing the binoculars away from his eyes, he wiped the beads of sweat forming on his brow with the back of his sleeve and began to peel back his gloves. A cloud of sand-filled dust whirled up from the ground in front of the trench, curling in waves as the wind swept it higher into the air. Layers of red dust were coated into his combats, making his body blend into the sandy banks either side of him. A deathly silence hung overhead and he leaned forward to pick up his weapon.

The stillness was shattered by a shout beyond the bank, immediately followed by the splatter of gunfire to his right. Crouching even lower and keeping his head down, he crawled to the other end of the trench, raising his gun to the gap in the sandbags and fixing his eye to the weapon's sights. His breath was coming more rapidly and he could feel the thump of his heart against his body armour. Staring out at the sea of sand and rocks, he heard his troop shuffling in behind him, and the radio crackled with curt instructions as more gunfire exploded in two directions.

Seconds later, a small band of dust-caked figures erupted into action, as a voice over the radio screeched, "Man down, man down!" Emerging from the trench, three soldiers began jogging toward a line of bushes, while rapid fire from the trench behind covered their progress. Shouts and gunfire seemed to be coming from all directions, and the distant whir of a helicopter began to get louder.

"Mark! Mark!" a voice was shouting above the gunfire. "Mark, where are you? Mark?"

I could still hear the voice screaming in my head when I woke up. I was trembling and instinctively reached out to touch the space in the bed beside me, which was empty, of course. It was my voice screaming. It was my nightmare. And I thought, *Mark, where are you?*

* * *

Downstairs I watched a steady curl of steam drifting up from the purring kettle. Everything seemed slow this morning, even the kettle. *And still no email.* I pushed the laptop away and began spooning a generous helping of coffee granules into my favourite spotty red mug. Balancing the coffee mug in one hand and my open laptop in the other, I padded upstairs, murmuring to myself through clenched teeth, "Come on, honey, email me... please." On the landing I caught a glimpse of Alix's peaceful face, bathed in the softest morning sunshine which was streaming in through a gap in her curtains. My breath caught in my throat at the sight. It was too early to get them up so I resisted the temptation to go in and stroke her perfect pale cheeks. *In any case*, I thought, *if he emails soon, I'll be able to tell them, "Daddy's coming home on Thursday."*

Laying the laptop on the bed, I couldn't stop myself leaning across and pressing "Send and receive" again. The file icons scrolled briefly before the words froze. No new emails. I sighed and headed for the shower.

What if? I thought, staring at my reflection in the mirror. Two vivid blue eyes gazed back at me. They were wary and there were dark shadows appearing below them – the result of too many restless nights when I'd dreamt of Mark walking across dusty fields or crouching behind sand-filled barricades, while gunshots echoed and helicopters whirred overhead. *Too many films, Brenda...* I could hear his voice in my head and smiled in spite of myself. "OK, big man," I said out loud, addressing the reflection. I reached for my toothbrush, talking sternly to myself as I squeezed a line of toothpaste onto the brush, and muttered, "I know this is the job you love, but it's so difficult being here and just waiting for news. We're the ones who need a medal..."

A sharp rap on the door below interrupted my lament. Quickly rinsing the froth from my mouth, I pulled on my dressing gown and headed downstairs to the front door. A sudden image of two uniformed soldiers standing grimly behind the door flashed into my head and I paused for a second with my hand on the latch, feeling my stomach somersault and my pulse race. I took a deep breath and pulled the door ajar, just enough to glimpse a blue and red uniformed postman grinning at me over the top of a large box. "Need a signature, please," and he pushed a digital handset toward me through the gap in the doorway. Shakily laying the parcel down in the hallway, I pulled the door closed, shook my head, and started to breathe more steadily.

"It's getting worse," I whispered. I'd never been so frightened that something would happen as I was on this particular tour.

I bent down to look more closely at the orange and white Amazon label, which read, "Mr M. Hale". *One of two possibilities*, I thought. *More rowing shorts or more likely something for the bike because it rattles. All the more reason for him to come back and inspect his orders.*

Back upstairs, I shrugged off the dressing gown, stepped back into the bathroom, and reached to turn on the shower. Above the noise of the water, I heard a short ping from the bedroom and immediately launched myself back toward the bed, grabbing the laptop.

The bold black type of a new message at the top of the screen, with the words "Mark Hale" in the "From" column, was the best thing I had seen in weeks. Clicking on the email, my eyes filled with tears as I read, "I'm in Bastion… hope you're ready for this!" I chuckled to myself and enjoyed that familiar yet delicious feeling of butterflies. "We're nearly there, Mark, just you wait!"

Seconds later I was singing raucously as the hot water showered down on me. "Thank you, Jesus," I said, and I couldn't resist clapping my hands and dancing on the warm tiles, chanting, "He's coming home, he's coming home! Hallelujah!"

Thursday morning

The scratches on the bumper of the blue car in front were clearly visible as we hugged its tail on the winding bends. Around the next corner a short stretch of clear road loomed, and I glanced in the rear-view mirror before pulling the steering wheel sharply to the right and crushing my foot on the accelerator. Just as I'd slid the car out onto the other side of the road, a lorry appeared ahead.

"****!" I said under my breath, as I veered back to tuck in on the right side of the road again behind the dawdling motorist. I couldn't help tapping my hand on the steering wheel. I sighed, "Oh come on, this is ridiculous," as I watched the needle on the speed dial flicker below thirty miles per hour.

Glancing in the rear-view mirror, I could see eight-year-old Alix, who was singing the French song *Alouette*, her head rocking from side to side. Beside her, a mop of curly golden hair hid her older sister's face as she was intent on scrolling through a series of text messages and chuckling to herself as she read them. As the bends continued to make overtaking impossible, I checked my own reflection and sighed at my pale cheeks. At least my hair was good and my nails had been done. *We might be late, but we'll be looking good for him,* I thought.

Half an hour later, a dust-ridden figure with a tanned face and piercing green eyes lounged in the passenger seat next to me. He was dressed in jeans and a T-shirt, but the shirt was crumpled and orange dust was visible in the creases. A grin was stretched across his face as he looked across at me, and I could hardly breathe. Sweeping the car round the country bends, my hands gripped the steering wheel.

"You're filthy, Mark," I said in a scolding voice, but I was smiling. It had been a tiny bit tense at first, because he was disappointed that we were late and we hadn't been able to meet him at the airport. The flight had been unexpectedly early, but the frustration of the long wait soon evaporated as he was pounced on by both girls and had swept all three of us into his arms. "Girly hugs!" he demanded, and there was a slight catch in his voice that we'd all wanted to ignore. Tears of joy had crept down my face and I'd wiped them away hastily.

Looking across at him, I could hardly believe he was there. It had been a long and difficult few months. "We need to get you to the barber's right now!" I said, trying to take my mind off all the emotion. "What a state you're in, Mark. I'm not letting you in the house like that."

He turned to the girls in the back. "What do you think, girls, you like my long hair, don't you?"

Alix just smiled sweetly at him. Tori leaned forward with a cheeky grin and said, "You could probably have a ponytail soon, Dad!"

They all laughed. Mark reached up, pulled his hair back behind his head and sucked in his cheeks. Leaning toward me, he said, "What d'you think? Is it sexy?" I giggled but slapped his leg anyway, and we were all laughing again.

As I emptied the dishwasher later, I could hear the thump of bags being dragged up the stairs. "Put your back into it, girls, that's pathetic." There was laughter and squeals, interrupted by the doorbell.

Wondering who it could be, I pushed the dishwasher door shut and strode to the front door, where I saw the kindly face of our next-door neighbour. He was holding out a large cake tin. "It's for Mark, to celebrate – I know he loves chocolate cake," he said.

"Ah thanks, Ian, that's so lovely." I hesitated, wondering if I should ask him in, but he was already nodding and turning away. "It's just to say 'Welcome home'. We're so proud of what he's doing out there. I don't want to interrupt…" And he was gone.

I stepped back inside. As I carried the cake into the kitchen, I could feel my hands shaking and a deep sob rose in my throat. I just managed to put the cake down on the table before the tears began racing down my face. Perhaps they were tears of relief, or maybe I was just overwhelmed at the unexpected kindness of a neighbour.

Wiping away the tears, I looked up as Mark came into the kitchen. "What's the matter?" he said, stepping toward me.

"Look what our neighbour did," I said, pointing to the huge chocolate cake. I knew he could hear the tremble in my voice.

He moved over and wrapped his arms around me until my sobs subsided. He stroked my hair and, kissing my head, whispered,

"I've missed you, Brenny, so, so much. You know I couldn't get through it without you."

I wanted to say the same, but no words came out. I just buried my head further into his chest, thinking I couldn't ever survive without this wonderful man in my life.

Half an hour later, I opened the bedroom door, a cup of tea in my hand. I noticed the damp towel discarded on the floor and the dusty jeans and T-shirt lying in a heap by the chair. My man was fast asleep, lying across the bed, his newly cropped dark hair a splash of black on the white pillows. His face looked peaceful, tanned, and slightly weathered. *He's lost weight*, I thought. Then and there, all I wanted to do was put the mug down, climb on the bed, and cuddle up next to him. But instead I pulled the door closed softly so as not to disturb him. *He needs to rest*, I thought. *At least in sleep he can escape those awful memories...*

CHAPTER 2

February 1985: Northern Ireland

... a time to dance

Blue, red, and green lights flashed across the darkened room, changing in time with the pulsating music. The dance floor was getting fuller by the minute as more and more couples stepped into the throng. With Madonna's "Like a Virgin" echoing around the club, I watched as a group of girls raised their arms and joined in the words, all sounding out of tune. I was standing to one side of the dance floor next to some other girls, leaning against the wall. We were all balancing glasses in one hand and handbags under our arms. I was half listening to a discussion between three of the girls, whom I vaguely knew from school, as they joked about a particular boy on the dance floor. Looking down at my tight white jeans, I swirled my drink against the sides of the tall glass.

Across by the bar I could see eager drinkers holding out £5 notes over a sea of shoulders as they attempted to attract the attention of the frantic barmen. There were plenty of broad-shouldered men with short-cropped hair and tattoos blazoned on their arms – *squaddie IDs*, I thought. I took another sip of my drink and shot a glance over at the dance floor, where various couples had begun to slow their movements in time with Lionel Richie's "Hello".

The words echoed in my head. I wasn't enjoying myself tonight. The music hadn't been great and now Nuala had disappeared somewhere. *The place is full of squaddies,* I thought... *and one particular squaddie too.* I didn't want him to know I was watching, but I couldn't help noticing him when I scanned the dance floor again for Nuala. His tall, dark figure seemed to stand out wherever it was – either fighting his way to the bar or pulling a girl toward him on the dance floor. It had been the same for the past few weeks.

I knew my dad would go mad if he were to find out I was at this club, which had a reputation as a hang-out for British squaddies. My parents had warned me about it because these places inevitably became terrorist targets. I could hear my father's voice: "I don't want you to be another bombing statistic on the news, Brenda." But Nuala had persuaded me that there were some really "hot-looking" boys and we should give it a try. That was four weeks ago and, inevitably, Nuala had met Jeff. As it wasn't easy or safe to date a soldier, she had persuaded me to go with her again.

He'd asked me to dance that night, but I later discovered it was just to get me out of the way while his mate Jeff made a move on Nuala. I had been impressed, but I didn't want him to know that. He was six feet four, dark and handsome with a soft Dorset drawl. He had a broad grin and his deep green eyes contained a mischievous twinkle. Taking his hand and following him onto the dance floor, I had felt my heart doing somersaults and told myself to calm down.

"What's your name?" I'd shouted as we swayed toward each other and were jostled by a throng of warm bodies either side.

"Mark," he'd said, and the cheeky smile crept across his face.

"Mark who?" I'd continued. I knew he was being deliberately cagey.

I asked what he did and he said he was a fireman from London.

"What are you doing in Bangor, then?"

He shrugged his soldiers and said, "I'm on holiday."

In January? I thought, and quickly retorted, "No, you're not. You're a soldier."

He shook his head gravely and said, "No, I'm not."

He had looked slightly annoyed then and glanced across to where Nuala was dancing with Jeff. As the song ended, he had mumbled something about going to the bar and I had moved back to where my friends were standing. Later I'd told Nuala he was arrogant – good-looking, but arrogant. And I'd heard the following week that he thought I had a bad attitude. So that was it – I definitely wasn't interested in him or whichever girl he was dancing with tonight.

Except I was.

* * *

Each week I couldn't help bumping into him. Either he would be coming out of the toilets and he would nod in acknowledgment, or I would catch his eye as he walked toward the bar. The previous week I'd been watching him as he danced and he had glanced across and seen me looking at him. It was embarrassing and I'd made Nuala leave quickly. But I also thought he'd been looking at me. I had definitely felt his gaze earlier tonight, and when I turned my head, our eyes met awkwardly.

Deep in thought, I felt an arm slide around my waist while a beery-breathed voice bellowed in my ear, "Another drink, Bren?"

I didn't really feel like any more to drink, but thought, *Why not?* I nodded back at Jeff and said, "Same again, please." *At least soldiers have money to spend and know how to look after a girl,* I thought.

I inched my way back to the wall and found a spot where I could view the dance floor unnoticed, shielded behind another group of girls. It wasn't long before I spotted him. He was in a particularly close clinch with a pretty girl with long, dark hair. I watched as his hands gripped her waist and then slid smoothly round her back as he drew her closer. It felt wrong and I wanted to shout at them to stop – it should be me he was dancing with, my waist he was gripping. The music had slowed right down and I couldn't take my eyes away from them as their heads began to move toward each other. I watched with a sinking feeling in my heart as their lips locked together and their bodies were pressed close. I felt my eyes fill with tears and hurriedly tried to wipe them away. *Idiot, don't be an idiot; he's just a stupid squaddie.*

Before I could get myself under control, another friend from the group, Symmo, was back from the bar with another drink. I felt his arm around my shoulders and he looked concerned. "What's up, Bren? What happened?"

I gulped and fought back a sob, as the unexpected touch had made me feel worse. Taking a sip of the new drink, I took a breath and found myself blurting out, "I fancy Mark but he's got a girlfriend... Please don't tell him."

Symmo looked shocked and glanced across to where his friend was entangled with the slim, dark-haired girl in a short skirt. He patted my arm and said, "Don't worry; I won't tell him."

Nuala appeared next to me then and gave me a hug as Symmo slipped away toward the dance floor. We headed for the toilets to fix our make-up and for me to sort out my emotions.

When we emerged, Mark was standing beside the door. It seemed as if he had been waiting for me to come out. When I looked up at him, that familiar feeling of butterflies dancing inside my stomach returned all over again. His short-cropped, dark hair made his eyes stand out even more, and he was looking directly at me with a slightly puzzled expression. "Do you fancy going out with me?" he said.

"What do you think?"

"I don't know, I really don't know."

I smiled then and said, "Yes, that would be good."

This time when he held out his hand, we were both smiling at each other, and he started to lead me onto the dance floor.

"Wait a minute," I said, pulling my hand free. "What about that girl you were dancing with? Isn't she your girlfriend?"

"I've just dumped her," he said. That wicked smile flashed across his face again as he pulled me into his arms and we moved into the swaying crowd.

* * *

I heard the footsteps as they crunched down the path, then that familiar clatter of the letterbox I had been waiting for. In a second I was out of bed, almost colliding with my dad, who was at the top of the stairs, already showered and dressed. He stepped back to let me dash past, calling after me, "He's a good letter writer... but he's still just a soldier, Brenda."

I crouched down and sorted through the envelopes on the mat in front of the door until I spotted the familiar handwriting addressed to "Miss Brenda Winters". I held the envelope to my lips and looked up at my dad, now hovering above me, a smile lighting up my face. "I know he's a soldier, Daddy. And he loves me too!"

He huffed and turned away, muttering as he moved toward the kitchen. I could hear him bustling in the cupboards and clattering cups.

I snuggled back beneath the duvet. It was a chilly morning but I could hear the radiators jangling and hissing, a signal that the heating was coming on. The unopened envelope lay on the covers in front of me and I savoured the moment of it being there. Mark was a good letter writer but sometimes, if he was on exercise, he couldn't get the letters to me, and inevitably there were gaps. I hadn't heard from him for a week now, and it felt like a very long time. I was hoping he might phone soon. There was so much to talk about.

That night on the dance floor when we had finally got together seemed a long time ago, but every time I saw those laughing green eyes my heart skipped a beat and I was lost. We'd only had ten weeks together before he left for a posting in Germany for two years. That had come as a bit of a shock after the first few dates. I'd been terrified of telling my parents I was dating a British soldier. Not only that, but he was a private soldier. I had imagined them asking what his prospects were. Dating soldiers in Northern Ireland was a risky business and could have put us all in danger from terrorist reprisals. I knew they wouldn't be happy when they found out. Each night when he walked me home, he'd say, "Shall I come in?" and I'd say, "Not yet."

In the end he said, "When am I going to meet your parents?" I knew I'd have to give in and introduce him. It was a Tuesday evening. We'd been in the pub and I couldn't put it off any longer, but I had to give them some warning. I told Mark I needed to ring home. Around the corner from the pub we squeezed into the empty phone box, leaving the door open a bit because it smelt so badly of urine and hot plastic. Mark was smiling as I fumbled for some change and began dialling the number. I turned my back on him, worried he'd make me giggle. My heart was thumping; I couldn't believe it was making me so nervous.

My mum answered and I told her I was bringing someone home. Then Mark was tapping me on the shoulder, and I put my hand over the receiver. "What?" I whispered.

He just took the phone from me and started talking. "I'm making sure your daughter gets home alright, Mrs Winters," he said in his Dorset drawl.

He's so English, there'll be no mistaking he's a soldier, I thought, as we turned up the path to the front door, where the highly polished brass letterbox winked at us encouragingly. It was a little before 11 p.m. and my parents were still up. The television was on in the lounge and my father stood up as we walked in. Mark stepped past me and held out his hand.

"This is Mark, Daddy," I said.

"Nice to meet you," he said, formally shaking his hand.

"Yer, cheers mate," Mark answered.

"Cheers mate!" I thought, and cringed inwardly. It wasn't quite the greeting I'd expect for my father. He was a very proper man – he even wore a shirt and tie on Saturdays, for goodness' sake! Mark sat down on the settee and the conversation quickly moved to football. Everything seemed amicable. *He's doing OK*, I thought as I sighed inwardly, so glad that my secret date was at last out in the open.

It wasn't long before there was a ring at the door, signalling the arrival of the taxi to take Mark back to the barracks. As I leaned against the closed door, my father appeared in the doorway. "You need to be careful, young lady," he said quietly, before moving away into the kitchen.

It was down to my mum to fill in the missing pieces, which she did that evening and the next morning over breakfast. I heard all about what happened to girls who married soldiers. They got pregnant and came back to Belfast and lived in council flats on benefits while their husbands were away. "That's not the kind of future we had planned for you, Brenda." She waved the breadknife at me before laying it down with a clunk on the breadboard.

I knew my dad thought it was just a phase. He was actually quite relieved when he heard Mark had been posted to Berlin. I heard him talking to my mum, saying I'd get over Mark. I shook my head as I touched the corners of the envelope, saying quietly to myself, "I'll never get over you, Mark Hale, no matter what happens."

He'd already given me a few scares. There had been the night of the bombing at Newry police station, where he was sometimes based. I'd seen it on the news and an awful fear had crept through me, starting deep down in the pit of my stomach. I'd sat on the edge of the settee, staring at the footage on the television of the bomb damage and listening to the details about the deaths and casualties, my body tense. Dad had glanced across at me. His dark hair was greying now, but it was still cut immaculately. He was wearing a dark cardigan over his shirt; his brown trousers, although not his best ones, still had a sharp crease down the middle. I'd heard him sigh. Then he'd asked abruptly, "Is that where your Mark works?" I had nodded, looking across at him. He must have seen the fear in my face because his eyes slid away, back toward the images on the screen. He didn't speak, but he shook his head fractionally. He didn't need to. I could hear the unspoken words in my head, *"I warned you, Brenda, that's what you get for dating a soldier – heartache. A life of heartache."*

My mum had been clattering plates in the kitchen, calling out that dinner was ready. I'd stood up shakily – I didn't feel hungry any more.

It was another couple of hours before Mark had phoned to tell me he was OK. I'd cried with relief – but I'd been a bit short with him on the phone. I didn't want him to realize how much it had frightened me.

It was different now. He'd already asked me twice to marry him, but there were days when I still couldn't believe he loved me.

I picked up the envelope and began to peel it open, pulling out a thick wodge of pages. It was Saturday, plenty of time to enjoy reading his letter.

Brenda, my darling, I am missing you so much...

There was a brief knock at the door and my mum stepped in, a cup of steaming tea in her hand. She smiled as she set down the tea on the bedside table. Glancing at the letter, she said, "How's Mark?"

"I haven't read it yet, Mum, but I'm sure he's fine. He's got leave in April. He wants me to go out to Germany."

I knew they weren't happy about me going out to Berlin. They would want to know where I was staying and what we'd be doing. But I'd be eighteen soon and Mark always paid for my flights to the UK. I had no money, so at least they knew he was looking after me – even if he had to put some of it on credit card. One of his mates had told me, "He saves like mad when you're not here, Brenda." Mark had been up at the bar getting drinks at the time. "He never goes out – he tells us he has to save for your flights, and to look after you when you come out."

Mum nodded and stroked my hair thoughtfully. "April? What, during the Easter holidays?" She paused. "We'll have to talk about it and see what your dad says. There's your college work to think about though..."

I turned away from her onto my side to continue reading the letter, saying, "Yes, I know. I'll be fine. I can work a bit while I'm there. Mark understands." I couldn't tell her we were planning to get engaged. I'd told Mark I could go to university in England, but I knew they wouldn't be happy about me getting married so young, and to a soldier. That was a battle for another day.

CHAPTER 3

July 1987: Bournemouth

... a time to love

I could hear a car moving slowly away below the window, taking my mother and the bridesmaids to the church. *Today's the day – it's finally arrived.* I looked down at my carefully painted nails and noticed the slight tremble running through my hands. The diamond and sapphire engagement ring sparkled in the sunlight and I twisted the band slowly, staring hard at the intricate setting. I'd fallen in love with the ring as soon as I'd seen it in the shop window.

"That one... definitely that one?" He sounded uncertain as he peered at the tiny price tag.

I leaned my head on his shoulder. "Shall we go in and have a look, then?" He slid his hands deeper into the pockets of his jeans. He was still looking hard at the array of sparkling rings on the stand. I looped my arm through his and gently steered him toward the door.

The assistant placed a small tray of rings on the counter in front of us. He was asking about my ring size and handed over a selection of plain metal rings held together by a clip for me to try for size. I slipped on a few other rings, but the one I liked best was the original one I'd spotted that was £175. I knew he thought it was a lot of money, *but surely I'm worth it?* We'd spent so many months writing and talking on the phone it seemed unreal that we were actually together.

The separation had been tough. When he had left for Berlin with his regiment, the 1st Battalion the Devonshire and Dorset Regiment (also known as the D&Ds), it was six months before he had come back. That October we'd spent a week in Bangor and then a week in Bournemouth, where I'd met his parents for the first time. Our life together seemed to be all about intense days spent with each other and emotional farewells. At the end of that leave we were both at Heathrow Airport, about to board separate flights – Mark to Berlin and me to Belfast. He'd asked me to marry him a few days before while we walked in the gardens in Bournemouth. That was the second time he'd asked. I'd shaken my head sadly and said, "I still think we're too young, Mark." He was only just eighteen and I was seventeen.

He had held my hand as we stared up at the departure board. "It's not so long, Brenda, only a few months till January… I'm not missing your eighteenth birthday!"

I'd wrapped my arms around his neck and felt the tears flood down my face. He'd gripped me tightly too and I could feel him shaking. When we had finally wiped our eyes and he'd heaved his huge bag over his shoulders, he'd waved as he turned away and I could see the tears welling in his eyes again.

A nun sitting nearby had smiled at me as I dried my eyes. "Your soldier boyfriend?" she asked. I shook my head: I didn't want to admit I was dating a soldier – Northern Irish habits die hard. She'd leaned across and patted my hand. "You'll be fine," she said.

I watched the light from the ring flashing on the bedroom walls beside me. It was a pretty ring. Mark had just completed the Berlin to Exeter marathon the week I'd picked it out. As we had walked out of the jewellery shop, I had been swinging the precious bag. I had sensed Mark increasing his stride as he made for the shop across the road, with a large blue and red sign above the doors. I'd felt a bit guilty about him spending all his money on a ring. But I was so happy, I barely noticed him studying the pages of the Argos catalogue and then jotting down numbers on a piece of paper as we joined the queue.

The next moment he was handing over even more than £175 to pay for the new weightlifting sets he'd just ordered. The culprits were still here, lurking in the corner under the window. The shiny silver poles and dark grey weights were some of his most prized possessions because he was fanatical about keeping fit and building up his muscle power. It hadn't been very long before I'd plucked up the courage to challenge the decision and ask him why it had been so hard for him to buy that ring, which hadn't even cost as much as his new weights.

"I guess I still couldn't believe you said 'Yes'. I was worried you might change your mind and it would all be a waste," he'd said. It had been an honest answer.

My eyes scanned the room. It wasn't my room: it was Mark's bedroom, the room we would be staying in after we were married. The line of mirrored wardrobe doors gave a strange perspective, reflecting the bed and a pile of green and khaki rucksacks and kit stacked in the corner. It was a reminder of what I was marrying into. In a few days my new husband would be leaving me for four months.

Things hadn't gone quite to plan, and maybe that was something I was going to have to adjust to in the years ahead. I was supposed to be getting married from my home in Northern

Ireland, but marrying a British soldier in Bangor was never going to be easy, or safe. At the last minute, security clearance had been withdrawn and the wedding had to be switched to the UK. I could still picture my mother's face when she heard – how could she arrange a wedding in England? So it had been down to Dianne, Mark's mother, to rally round and pull things together. Somehow it had been sorted.

Ever since our engagement the previous April, I'd been on a rollercoaster ride. Now I'd reached the final climb on the loop and the big exhilarating drop was just ahead. A month earlier I had been saying goodbye to friends on the last day at college. Some of them were heading to university, others to jobs or further training. None of them was getting married.

I stared down at the delicate pattern on the white fabric of my dress. I remembered watching my mum folding it gently into the box a few weeks earlier, tears glistening in her eyes. The next day I would be leaving home to fly to Bournemouth where Mark and I would be married six weeks later. "I don't want anyone to be here tomorrow... before I go... Mummy," I had said, a slight catch in my voice.

A frown had creased her forehead. "Your dad will be at work. I'm not sure what the others are doing. I thought..."

"I need you to go out with the others. Make sure there's no one here... please, I don't want to get upset."

She didn't like it, but she'd agreed.

The next morning I had finished packing my suitcase in the empty house in Bangor. I had turned over the small folded note I'd found on the kitchen table. It was from my mum, to say she loved me and that she'd see me in a couple of weeks. Tears had started to well up in my eyes again and I'd brushed them away. *I'm not going to cry*, I thought. I had given a last look round the room that had been my teenage refuge for the last few years and inhaled deeply. It had been decorated to my taste with a navy carpet, white walls, and a blue and white flower-patterned duvet. The bed was under the window, and it was there I had waited every day for letters from my beloved Mark. The little lamp had sat beside my radio and there was a space now where there had been a framed photograph of Mark. That was safely in my suitcase, along with other essentials.

In the hallway downstairs, I had picked up the huge cardboard box with my wedding dress in it and slammed the front door behind me, closing off that chapter of my life. As I had loaded my belongings into the car outside, I'd glanced back at the front of the house, taking in its pebble-dashed walls and front door with the leaded glass window and shimmering brass letterbox, which my mother polished religiously each week. The garden was awash with colour as petunias, candy canes, lobelia, and giant daisies tumbled over one another, fighting their way toward the path. The garden was my father's pride and joy. I had gulped down the sob that was rising in my throat and fixed an image of Mark's dancing eyes in my head. Although I was sad to be leaving the little house that had been my home for as long as I could remember, and the safety of my family and friends, I was going to be with the man of my dreams.

It was a bit frightening today too, but I also felt a tremor of excitement. I was about to start a new life with that handsome stranger I'd met at the disco. He would be waiting for me now at the church down the road. I didn't know what lay ahead, and I didn't mind, as long as I would be with Mark.

I heard the bathroom door click shut and glanced behind me to see my father standing in the bedroom doorway. His smile was a little weak – I knew he was still worried about me marrying Mark and not going to university as planned. He came in and sat on the end of the bed. I snatched up a tissue as I stared into the mirror and dabbed at the lipstick, wondering if I'd put on too much. *He's going to ask me again*, I thought.

I heard him gently clear his throat. "Brenda, is everything OK? Are you alright?"

I reached out, held his hands in mine, and looked into his eyes. "Everything is fine, Daddy, and I'm so happy right now."

He squeezed my hands and said, "You look beautiful."

A car door banged outside and there was a brisk knock on the door. I stood up and brushed down the folds in the delicate white dress. On the other side of the room, reflected in a long mirror, I caught sight of a slim, blonde-haired girl in a flowing white dress, the veil pulled back to reveal her features. Her blue eyes looked wide and slightly startled, but there was a determined set to her head, and an excited flush had crept across her cheeks. *This is me – on my wedding day.* I gave a little sigh and then I laughed. "Come on, Daddy, we'd better get going. You can smile, too – it's my wedding day, not my funeral!"

In the car he gripped my hand. As I was settling back in the seat, having rearranged the folds in the billowing skirt, he turned toward me. "Brenda."

I looked up into his watery eyes. I nodded; I couldn't speak.

"You know I want you to be happy. Are you sure about this? You don't have to do it – it's not too late to change your mind."

I knew he thought it would be better if Mark were to leave the army and get another job. He wanted me to go to university and he thought I was throwing away the possibility of a bright career. I was my daddy's golden girl – I knew this was a tough call for him.

I looked into his eyes so that he'd know I meant it. "You don't have to worry. I love Mark with all my heart, and today I'm going to marry him. I'll go to university just as soon as we've got ourselves established. It's going to be OK. You don't have to worry about me: it's going to be fine."

But inside I was worried. Not worried that I was about to marry the wrong person, or that I was making a mistake by moving to England. Instead, I was scared to death that this wonderful man might change his mind and not want to marry me. What if he didn't turn up?

* * *

"I, Brenda, take you, Mark, to be my husband… for better for worse, for richer for poorer, in sickness and in health… till death do us part."

My eyes were fixed on his as I murmured the words after the vicar. Even in my heels he towered above me, looking more dashing than ever in his number two uniform with its thick leather belt and brassy buttons. A broad grin was beginning to spread across his face. He slid the ring onto the end of my finger and gave my other hand a reassuring squeeze as the vicar's words boomed out across the church.

It was Mark's turn to speak again now. He looked deep into my eyes as he echoed the words of the vows. "I give you this ring as a sign of our marriage… With my body, I honour you."

At this point he grinned more broadly and winked. I giggled and a ripple of laughter spread across the congregation. As we sat down and the vicar began to pray, Mark whispered in my ear, "I'm glad you turned up!"

He was incorrigible. He loved to make a joke in the most serious moments and make me laugh. But I knew he was trying to help me relax and break the tension. His strong hand lay over mine and I watched as he played with the rings, twisting them around, until I pulled my hand away. I looked up at him, aware of all our family and friends in the rows behind us. His green eyes sparkled and there was a smile quivering on his lips. *He loves me*, I thought, and part of me still couldn't really believe it…

The previous two and a half years had passed in a flash and we'd hardly spent more than a few weeks together in total. We'd had to get to know one another through letters and phone calls. Sometimes he would write three times a day, while I was studying and trying to earn money by babysitting whenever I could. I'd flown out to Berlin that summer after we'd got engaged, and the weeks apart had felt like an eternity. Mum and Dad had thawed toward Mark by then, and once we were engaged, flying out to Berlin hadn't been such an issue. They had got to know him a little more each time he had visited.

I pictured the night he'd proposed to me, in the same club where we'd met a year earlier. He had saved up hard to fly back for my eighteenth birthday in January and join in the family celebrations. Later we'd gone to a disco with Nuala and his best friend Jeff. Mark told me later that he'd decided to ask me to marry him again, after I'd agreed that I could go to university in England instead of in Northern Ireland. His regiment was due to be posted back from Berlin the following year to an army base at Bulford in Wiltshire, and he had researched which universities were within reach.

The music in the disco was loud that night and there was a strong beat that seemed to make my heart drum. I nestled my head against his shoulder as we sat in a dark alcove by ourselves. I smiled as I recalled our first dance together, and then I felt him move away from me slightly. He placed his drink on the table in front, turned toward me, and whispered in my ear, "Brenda."

He sounded different, a little serious, and my heart skipped a beat.

"I think we should get married." His eyes were fixed on mine. This was the third time he'd asked me, and this time it felt right.

There was only one word I needed to say. "Yes," I said, smiling into his eyes, "I think we should."

"Good," he said. "Because that was the last time I was going to ask you!"

* * *

A few weeks later he flew back to visit me in Belfast for a week. He'd bought me a rowing machine and squeezed it into a space on the landing. It was a present for me, but he was using it! I could hear the machine squeaking and his breathing becoming louder as the speed increased. It was the holidays and I wanted to go shopping, but he'd said we shouldn't go because we needed to save money for my flight to Berlin in the summer. We'd been discussing it for a while and I wasn't giving up easily. I called up to him again, saying we could get the bus and go. I was used to getting my own way with boyfriends, and even with Mum and Dad. I could usually persuade them to come round to what I wanted.

"Mark, come on," I shouted over the noise of pulleys. "Pleeeaase... I really want to go."

He paused just long enough to say, "No, Brenda, and I mean No."

He was very disciplined and he wasn't going to let me change his mind. Both my parents had heard the response and, as I turned away defeated, I heard my dad say to my mum, "She'll marry him." He knew I needed someone who would stand up to me.

As I looked up at Mark standing beside me in the church, I felt so lucky. I was the luckiest girl in the world. Neither of us could stop smiling and laughing as we paused at the top of the aisle, facing our beaming friends and family. He threaded my arm through his and we began to step forward slowly as the organ blasted out its celebration. I was thinking, *I still can't believe he chose me.*

*"He knew just how far to push it
and would only ever overstep the mark knowingly
and armed with an instantly forgivable grin."*

Major (now Lieutenant Colonel) Darren Denning

CHAPTER 4

December 1987: Poole, Dorset

... a time to begin

"Is that it? Surely that must be the last one?" I asked, wiping the perspiration from my forehead.

He leaned his weight on the tower of boxes and fixed me with his steady gaze. "That's the last of your shoes, Brenda. I've just got to pick up my weights and other kit across from the garage."

I must have looked dismayed because he gave another of his false cheesy grins. It was hard to get mad with him. He looked so handsome even in his scruffy jeans and torn T-shirt, his broad shoulders stretching the material taut. I'd been working all hours and felt quite exhausted.

"But Mark, where's it all going to go? It's only a small flat... I think you'd better wait and see. We need to unpack some more of these boxes first."

The main room was now jammed with towers of cardboard boxes. It was a scene that would be very familiar in the years to come, but this was our first flat. We'd scraped and saved over the past six months while Mark had been away. It hadn't been easy, but he kept telling me it would be worth it so that we could have our own place and not have to live in a quarter patch with other soldiers and their wives. He was always so protective. "I don't want you anywhere near the blokes, Brenda, it's not nice," he'd said.

For the first six months of our marriage we'd lived with Dianne and Roger, Mark's mother and stepfather. This meant we had paid out less on rent, which helped us save for our first mortgage on the flat. Dianne had told Mark she would look out for me as well, because almost immediately after the wedding Mark had been away for four months in the Falkland Islands. That had been hard, being apart immediately after getting married. Suddenly I was alone and, although I was in the house with my in-laws, I missed Mark more than ever. He wrote to me, often every day, but communication was difficult and sometimes there would be a week or two without anything, then a pile of "blueys" would arrive all at once, usually when a ship or a flight came in. Then I would lie in bed with a hot drink and savour each word, dreaming of him lying next to me.

I had also been doing my best to make money. I'd taken a job as a nursing auxiliary at a local nursing home. The pay was pretty low, so there wasn't much left after I'd paid my way in the house. However, my bosses, Penny and Rod Taylor, helped us to secure our mortgage – but only after a parental chat with us both to ensure that we were able to meet our payments. Meanwhile, Mark had been saving all he could, trying to live on £5 a day. I would save up and then make a trip into town and buy simple things like a new bath towel. Now the money was still tight but at least we were together in our own flat. It would be a long commute for Mark to Bulford each day, but he said it was worth it.

Mark surveyed the room slowly and then surprised me by giving in and saying, "OK, let's start unpacking some of this and I can go back later or tomorrow for the garage things, when we've got rid of a few boxes. Have you found the kettle yet?"

I'd kept it out deliberately and was quite proud of myself. Reaching across a pile of boxes, I picked up the brand new kettle from where it was balanced on a set of shelves, then I started to giggle. "We have a kettle and our bed, so I guess all is not lost..."

Footsteps on the stairs signalled the arrival of two of Mark's army mates who'd been helping us with the move. They appeared in the doorway a second later, one leaning against the door frame, staring at all the boxes. "Got enough stuff here for two houses, let alone a flat!"

The other friend chuckled too, shaking his head.

"Anyone want a cuppa?" I asked, waving the kettle in their direction.

"Well, as you're asking..."

A second after I'd squeezed my way toward the sink, I turned back toward them. "Could one of you pop down the road for teabags and milk, though?" as I gave them all that blameless beaming smile.

* * *

It didn't feel like Christmas; it was too warm. But I wriggled further down the bed, wanting to prolong this moment of waking up on Christmas morning next to my man. Having moved in a few weeks earlier, we were both still loving the novelty of having our own little home – a place to be together with no one else to answer to. The bedroom was very small; in fact, it was really part of the lounge, but Mark had got to work quickly after we'd unpacked some of the boxes. With help from his stepfather, Roger, he had managed to put up a partition so we had a separate space to sleep in. It had been a bit of a crush with them both working away, sawing and drilling things in such a small space. Dianne and I had stayed out of the way, making sandwiches in the kitchen. At least the curtains were new and the bed was a wedding present. *Who cares that we don't have a washing machine?* I looked at my broken nails. Hand-washing clothes was taking its toll, and even now I was thinking about the clothes dripping dry over the bath.

The previous day had been perfect. I'd finished work early and Mark was already on leave. It was our first Christmas Eve being married and living in the same place after all those months and months of separation. I could hardly believe it was real. When I got home I could see Mark had cleaned up the flat a bit and done the washing-up. He'd been shopping too, so we had some food. We had no spare money. It was all going on the mortgage, and there was only just enough for us to pay the bills and buy basic food for the week. We'd both agreed no presents this year. *The flat is our Christmas present*, we'd said. There were a few little parcels from family and friends above the fireplace, but we didn't care – we had each other and that was more than enough. We'd debated about spending on a Christmas tree and decided we couldn't afford it this year – thankfully we'd be at Mark's parents' for Christmas lunch.

I dropped my bag onto a chair and started to chuckle. Mark was smiling too. "I can't believe we're allowed to do this… be all on our own in our own flat on Christmas Eve!"

He stood up, a wide grin splitting his face and one arm held behind his back. As he stepped toward me, he waved it triumphantly. "Mistletoe, I have mistletoe!"

We were both laughing as he pulled me into his arms. As we fell onto the bed I told him we didn't need mistletoe. "You shouldn't have bought it; it's expensive."

"I didn't buy it. The lady in the shop slipped it into the shopping. She said, 'A nice looking lad like you might be needing this later!'"

That night we'd planned to meet up with friends at the pub. I heard the taxi beep down below as I slid my feet into a pair of navy court shoes. Teetering in my heels, I inched my way to the taxi on the road. Mark was bending down, speaking to the driver through the open window. He opened the door for me and then slapped his back pocket. "Hang on, Brenda, I've forgotten my wallet."

I sighed, but I was too happy to be annoyed.

"I won't be a sec," he said, and I watched him stride back toward the entrance to the flat.

Much later, when we tumbled out of another taxi, we were laughing as we wove our way up the stairs and Mark fumbled with the key in the lock. Before he pushed the door open, he turned to me and said, "Happy Christmas, Brenda... I wonder what Santa's brought you!"

He tasted of beer but I didn't mind, and I murmured, "Happy Christmas" too, thinking to myself, *You're my Christmas present – thank you, Santa.*

When I walked in, there was something strange about the lounge. A big pillowcase with red writing on it was slumped beside the fireplace. I stared and then looked at Mark, who was grinning. "Go on, have a look," he said, as he nudged me forward.

I tugged the material out flat and read the words in familiar but rather wobbly painted writing: "Happy Christmas, Brenda, lots of love, Santa." The improvised sack was bulging with strange shapes, and my eyes filled up. I looked up at him and said, "But we weren't doing presents, Mark, we agreed..."

He shrugged and said, "It's Santa, so it doesn't count." He crouched down beside me and said, "Go on then, see what's inside. It's Christmas Day now, so you can open it."

I paused, still holding the edge of the pillowcase. "This wasn't here when we left. How did you...?" He was smiling as he slid his arms around my waist and rested his head on my shoulder. Then

I remembered the dash back inside from the waiting taxi.

"You didn't forget your wallet at all, did you? Mark! You came back for the sack, didn't you? Where was it, where did you hide it?"

"Too many questions, Brenda. Open your presents… hurry up!"

"But…" He started tickling me so I wriggled from his grasp and felt inside for the packages. The first one I pulled out was a box of chocolates. Inside the largest parcel was a pair of white leather boots. I screamed as I opened the box and then kissed him, my arms wrapped round his neck. The smallest parcel was a bottle of my favourite perfume. It was perfect. Completely perfect.

I gazed at the presents piled on a chair in the corner where I'd left them the previous evening. He must have planned it for some time, and I still couldn't work out how he had saved enough money to buy them all. We had so little money left each month. I turned onto my side to look at him. His eyes were shut and his dark lashes lay like a lace frill against his cheeks. I traced my finger along his lips and he stirred. It was unfair to wake him because I would be going off to work soon for a few hours in the nursing home, where half of the residents would hardly know it was Christmas. I glanced at the clock: *Five more minutes of bliss.* Shuffling further toward him, I edged myself into the curve of his body, wishing I hadn't agreed to go into work on Christmas Day.

August 1988: France

Rhythmic pings and bleeps interspersed with synthesized piano music pulsated round the car. Mark's legs were stretched out beside me, toward the front seats, and I turned onto my side. Resting my head against the hot vinyl of the seat, I watched the other cars streaming past the window. Nigel Moreland was sitting in the front passenger seat, jigging from side to side and drumming his fingers on the dashboard, in time with each strange zing from the Jean-Michel Jarre track blaring out of the CD player. His older brother, Andy, one of Mark's best mates in the regiment, gripped the wheel and said he was starting to feel sick and might have to pull over soon to throw up if that awful noise didn't stop.

As the track came to an end, Andy snatched up another CD from the dashboard. The plaintive voice of Elvis Presley singing "Are you lonesome tonight?" began to swirl round the car and Andy began warbling along to the song, slightly out of tune. The agreement was for the brothers to alternate tracks of their favourite songs, but as another Elvis tune blasted out, Nigel's hand was swiped away from the CD player by Andy. "Leave it! Everyone's had enough of your music."

I felt the car lurch as Andy moved his arm to block a punch from his brother. We swerved across into the next lane, narrowly missing a car and caravan, which hooted loudly from behind us. The fight in the moving car was in full swing as Mark leaned forward to restrain Nigel while I protected Andy from behind, and we both shouted at them to stop before they killed us all.

A few minutes later, peace was restored for five minutes while the radio was switched on instead. Mark slid his arm around my shoulder and pulled me against him, squeezing my arm gently. He was shaking slightly and I realized he was trying to control his laughter. He loved these two brothers as if they were his own, but they were chalk and cheese, and the arguments continued all the way to the next little French town, where the search for a petrol station took priority over the choice of music. The little Peugeot 205 was doing well considering it had three hulking men in it, plus all our camping gear and me.

A working petrol pump was eventually found, and then the search began for a campsite. This proved to be even more controversial: too expensive, too many trees, too crowded. It was getting late, we all needed to get out of the car and I'd definitely had enough of driving on all those winding roads, chosen in order to avoid paying expensive tolls on the French motorways. Over the next ridge, as Andy, now in the passenger seat, was flicking through a campsite book, we spotted the Mediterranean glistening in the early evening light.

"The sea, the sea… I see the sea…" three of us chorused. With spirits roused, we headed straight for it and found a beautiful sandy cove about fifteen minutes later. The light was fading and, as the beach was almost empty, we decided to put off the search for a campsite until the next morning. While the three men started hunting out sleeping bags and mats in the overladen car, I wandered down to the shoreline, slid off my sandals, and let the cool waves crumble over my feet. It was just a year earlier that we had said "I do" and now I was Mrs Hale, wife of a Lance Corporal, soon to be a full Corporal, we hoped.

I watched as a lone fisherman swung his line out into the water as he perched on a rock at the entrance to the little cove. The sun was beginning to sink toward the horizon and its rays of gold, orange, and pink shot out across the water like an exotic cocktail. I glanced back at the men, jostling with one another now as they crouched over a small gas burner where they were cooking something up. I wasn't sure what it would taste like. *Probably army rations, knowing them*, I thought. *Never mind about the food, Brenda*, I said to myself. *There's a beach, it's hot, and I'm with Mark.*

* * *

The light shirt felt prickly on my back and I wished I'd been a bit more careful while sunbathing the previous day. In the cloudy mirror in the campsite shower I'd seen pale strap marks standing out against decidedly pink skin. I'd hitched up the damp towel and washbag, pushed a strand of wet hair away from my eyes, then squelched in my flip-flops along the gravel path. We'd settled on this campsite after a night sleeping on the beach. None of us had got much sleep there.

Winding my way between the haphazard layout of tents, I eventually spotted our little green one. It was pitched next to a sprawl of canvas between the trees, which was the Moreland brothers' contraption. When we'd arrived at the site, Mark and I had clipped poles together and unwound guy ropes, while the Morelands had pulled everything out of the car in search of tent poles. Their father, who was an ex-marine, had given them the tent. There were more arguments over who was at fault for packing a tent without poles, and a lot of pushing and shoving continued as the canvas was stretched between tree branches in an attempt to make a shelter.

Mark and Andy were crouched around the little stove when I arrived back. "Just in time for breakfast!" Andy called across to me as I draped my towel over one of the ropes attached to the trees.

"A cup of coffee would be great," I said, peering down at the dubious mixture in the pan.

Mark held up a spoonful of the brown speckled mixture for me to smell.

I pulled away and made a face. "What is it?"

He was spooning it onto the plastic plates. "Scrambled eggs and beans."

I snatched the fourth plate away and said I'd wait for Nigel to arrive with the fresh bread, thanks.

As I munched on my French stick and jam, the others were spooning in mouthfuls of brown scrambled egg. "You're too fussy, Brenda," said Andy as he gulped down another mouthful, gesturing with his spoon. "This is great slop. Our army chefs would be proud."

"Thankfully I'm not in the army," I retorted.

"Well, you sort of are…" chipped in Nigel.

Mark laid his plate on the grass and chuckled. "I've always said she only married me for my passport."

I squeezed his thigh and said, "Listen, mate, I have your pension now as well!"

Nigel was laughing too. "That's true, Mark," he said, "so if you poison yourself with this awful food, she'll be OK!"

Within a few days we had a reputation on the site. We were the only English there and some of the other campers had developed a soft spot for us, referring to us as *les Anglais* and various other names. We joined them at boules on the rough ground before the sand dunes, and although our French was barely more than "Franglais", there was plenty of banter and laughter.

Our funds were dwindling, and one evening we discovered a Vietnamese restaurant where we could eat as much as we wanted for just a few francs, so we returned each evening to the same place. I was sick of rice and noodles by the end of the week, but none of us complained.

The restaurant owner grinned at us from behind the counter as we pulled out the plastic chairs around a small table. Out of the corner of my eye I saw him nudge his daughter and signal for her to come and take our order. She was very slight and couldn't have been more than fifteen. She barely looked at us as she jotted down the drinks order on her notepad before scurrying away into the kitchen.

"Food good, boys?" The beaming owner was standing beside us and he patted Nigel on the back. "No wife yet?" he asked him. "You no find French wife?"

Nigel spluttered on his noodles as we all grinned at him.

"He's waiting for someone special, see," said Andy mischievously. "A really special girl… do you know any?"

The man was nodding excitedly. "Yes, yes... special girl... you like beautiful girls?" And he glanced over his shoulder, scanning the restaurant for his daughter.

Mark was looking over his beer at Nigel, who was moving the food around his plate awkwardly.

The owner was calling across at his wife now, obviously asking in rapid Vietnamese where his daughter was. Nigel looked meaningfully at Andy and shook his head.

The owner bent down and whispered something in Nigel's ear, then grinned again at us and hurried off in the direction of the kitchen. We all started laughing, except Nigel, who said, "I'm not hungry any more, and I think we should go – now!"

Several beers later we all arrived back at the campsite in the dark, and Andy stumbled over a bundle of objects propped beside the tent. "What's all this? What idiot left the milk out again?"

We peered down as Mark shone a torch beam to reveal a pile of food and a couple of loo rolls with a scrappy note attached, saying "*Bonnes vacances!*"

I smiled. "It must be from that couple in the little orange tent who were leaving... you know, Claude and – I don't know her name."

"Beer would have been better," muttered Nigel, as he stumbled toward the entrance of his makeshift tent.

CHAPTER 5

1 9 9 0 : D o r s e t

... a t i m e t o b e l i e v e

Bacon was sizzling under the grill, filling the kitchen with the promise of breakfast, while Mark was leaning against the sink, sipping tea. We'd driven over from our flat to spend the day with Andy Moreland and his new wife Kathy. They were living at Andy's parents' house in the heart of the Dorset countryside, instead of the army quarters at Bulford. It was Saturday morning and one of the few days when Andy refused to pull weights. Mark would have had them working out every day, but Andy insisted Saturdays were a day off from their usual weightlifting routine.

He always seemed to know we'd be ready for a meal. I suppose he guessed we were struggling to pay the bills each week, especially since the interest rate had started to rise on the mortgage. Meals could be a bit spartan at times as we only had about £12 to spend on our weekly shop. The previous day we'd gone round Kwik Save where I'd picked out the cheapest sausages, trying to save enough money to get a *Daily Telegraph*. That was our Saturday treat. Keeping the car going was draining our income too, but we couldn't do without it because Mark was commuting a hundred miles each day from Poole to where the regiment was based at Bulford.

"Is everyone hungry?" Andy called out over his shoulder as he cracked another egg into the sizzling oil.

"Starving," said Mark.

Kathy was slicing bread expertly. I moved next to her and began coating each slice with a smear of butter.

"That's a stingy amount, Brenda," she said, nudging me. "Is Mark worried about cholesterol or something?"

I chuckled softly. "His body is a temple, don't you know? Of course not. I'm just used to making everything go round so we have enough money to pay the flipping mortgage."

Andy chuckled. "At least you're getting a meal this morning."

"Too right," Mark chipped in. "Why else d'you think we're here?"

As I reached across to lay the plates around the table by the window, Kathy set down the buttered bread. "But you like the flat, don't you?" she asked.

I nodded. "It's so good to have our own place."

"You're lucky, Brenda. You don't have to live in the middle of the goldfish bowl in an army quarter."

It still seemed strange that Andy had returned from New Zealand married. His new wife, Kathy, was a calming influence and nothing seemed to ruffle her. She was often quietly organizing him behind the scenes. In some ways, we were complete opposites. She was so quiet. She'd sit happily without speaking. Mark was the quieter one in our relationship, but that meant when he did speak, people listened.

I shuffled into a chair by the window and stared out on the lush garden with its colourful shrubs and swaying trees. A narrow, paved path ran round in a curve before it disappeared behind a thick laurel hedge. There were scarlet geraniums in neatly arranged pots around the terrace. A drooping yellow rose had wound itself around the arch of a trellis over the path and an ornamental pond was shimmering blue, reflecting the clear sky above.

"It might be a nice day for a picnic," I said dreamily.

"Or a bike ride," said Mark and Andy, almost simultaneously.

Andy and Kathy were great friends and we had a lot of fun with them, but they were different to us. I didn't fully understand it but there was something... something very solid, something that gave them a deep confidence. I wanted to brush it aside because I was really happy being married to Mark, yet some of the things Andy had been saying lately made me feel as if something was missing.

Their friendship went back to when Mark had first joined the D&Ds. They had hit it off immediately and although Andy had been more senior, a strong bond had developed. They were part of the same platoon – the Recce platoon – which had the role of gathering intelligence and leading covert tasks on operations. They were also both into keeping fit and loved the adrenaline rush of getting out of sticky situations when they were out on the town. Andy had known Mark longer than he had known me, in fact, but I never felt excluded... except for one occasion the other week. I'd gone to tell them dinner was ready and it had been unusually quiet in the garage. Instead of the squeak of the rower or the huff and clank of weights, there was a low murmur of conversation. I paused at the corner of the house, wondering what they were talking about. I had an uneasy feeling as I pulled the door open. Their voices dropped and fell silent and I peered round to see them both sitting on the weights bench, leaning forward. Mark's face looked confused.

"Grub's up... if you're hungry, that is," I said.

Andy grinned and smacked Mark's leg. "Great. We needed a break, didn't we, mate?"

I felt as if I'd interrupted something, and uncertainty quivered in the base of my stomach again. *Were they talking about us? Is something wrong?* I planned to ask Mark later; I didn't want there to be any secrets between us. Now the banter over breakfast was as reassuring as ever, and I told myself I must have imagined something strange was going on.

* * *

I closed the book shut with a snap and pushed it away from me across the table, as if the words would disappear if I moved it away. "I am the way and the truth and the life… whoever loves his life will lose it… knock and the door will be opened…"

The phrases were echoing round my head, and Bible passages I'd heard in my childhood crowded in, one after another. That familiar image of Jesus, with dark, sad eyes, dressed in a long, white gown, holding a lamp, and standing beside an overgrown door without a handle, seemed as clear as if the painting was hanging above the fireplace.

Andy had spoken to us about his new-found Christian faith. We'd all been shocked when he'd come back from New Zealand a changed man, and it wasn't just because he'd got married. We'd both seen a change in him and he said God had told him to come back into the army to tell his friends about his faith. This seemed a little far-fetched to most of us, but Andy was a lovable guy and so we put up with his eccentricities. I'd been brought up to go to church; after all, I'd lived in Northern Ireland. I'd been in the Girls' Brigade and the church youth fellowship, and I'd gone to church most Sundays. I certainly knew all the stories, but I'd never given my heart to it – never known what it was to talk to God, except in a crisis.

I hadn't been looking for any answers either. Life was good. I loved my job and I was married to Mark and I thought that was all I needed, most days. But Andy didn't let us forget about God. Somehow he couldn't help talking about Him at every opportunity. I only accepted the book to shut him up really, and then I'd started reading it on a quiet shift at work. It was called *The Truth Twisters*, and it looked at various religions and what they believed, in comparison with the Christian faith. The book kept asking questions which I couldn't answer. Words from the book were filling my head and I knew something was happening. I couldn't run from it any more. I reached to pick it up again, happy that I was alone in the flat and there was no chance of Mark coming back early from his training course. I wondered about taking the step of faith the book talked about. *Could it really be that simple? Would God really forgive me? And is He interested in me with all my failings?*

* * *

A few days later the smell of roast chicken was wafting up from the oven. *Surely it must be cooked by now*, I thought, as I nudged open the door to be met by a wave of heat. I was pleased to see that the roast potatoes were crisping beautifully and I turned my attention back to the gravy, while the sumptuous bird sat resting on the worktop. I felt Mark's arms slide around my waist seductively while he rested his chin on my head. "Smells delicious, Mrs Hale. When will it be ready?"

"I hope you're hungry, because there's masses now your mum and Roger aren't coming."

"Sunday roast – my favourite. Fancy a beer?"

He moved toward the fridge as I arranged the plates and cutlery on the little table by the window. I noticed a small stack of books stashed at one end of the sofa beside the wall; they didn't look like the normal military reading matter. I was sure one was entitled *Understanding Religion*. It seemed an odd choice of reading for Mark.

I heaved a sigh of relief as I gazed down at our plates, which were laden with chicken, stuffing, and vegetables, although I realized I hadn't been very generous on my portions of potatoes. It wasn't long before I'd finished my potatoes, and I looked longingly across at the last mouth-watering roastie on Mark's plate. It would go so well with my final piece of chicken and greens. "Can I have that potato?"

He blinked and stared down at the lone specimen before looking back at me and rearranging his face into a lopsided smile. He pushed his plate toward me and said, "OK, it's yours."

As I speared the potato with my fork, I knew something was wrong. Mark would never let me have his food, particularly not his roast potatoes. Mark didn't share food!

When I'd finished, I laid my cutlery neatly on the plate and stared across at him. "What's happening, Mark?"

"What d'you mean?"

"What's happened to you? Why did you let me have that potato? Is something wrong?"

He shifted in his chair uncomfortably and then pushed himself away from the table and gazed out of the window. He was scaring me now. Then he turned back and placed his hands on the table, palms down, as if he was about to confess something.

He cleared his throat. "Brenda…"

I could feel my heart thudding loudly and I caught my breath as I stared into his eyes. I was terrified about what was coming next.

"Do you remember a few weeks ago when we were at Andy and Kathy's – we had lunch with them in the garden and I was doing weights with Andy in the garage?"

I nodded silently, feeling puzzled.

"When I do weights, I can't help the odd swear word slipping out. Anyway, I told him I felt bad when I swore in front of him, and he said, 'You don't feel bad swearing in front of me, mate, it's the Holy Spirit making you feel bad.' Then he said, 'Don't take it from me; read about it for yourself.' Anyway I got all those books." He glanced across at the pile of books on the floor. "I've been reading all about different religions: Islam, Judaism, Jehovah's Witnesses, and the Bible. I was trying to find out if there's any truth in it and if what Andy said is true, about the Christian God being the only God, and about Him sending Jesus to earth. It makes sense. I know it makes sense."

Then he paused and turned the beer glass in his hand. "The thing is, every time I sit down I keep getting this verse, 'Be still and know that I am God', and I feel guilty, so I just read a bit more."

It was my turn to clear my throat and he paused. "Go on," I said.

He lowered his voice, as if he was imparting a dreadful secret. "He's right, Brenda. What Andy said is true. I... I've become a Christian. It's amazing. That's why I let you have my potato – because I'm changing. I don't want to just think of myself. I'm a different person now."

I was relieved and scared all at the same time. I gave a tentative smile and reached across the table to hold his hand.

"What are you thinking, Brenda? Do you think I'm mad?"

I shook my head. I was finding it hard to speak as a wave of emotions ran through me. I wanted to explain about my own journey for the past few weeks. "It is amazing... I... it's happened to me as well, Mark. That book Andy gave me – I've been reading it on my night shifts. A couple of weeks ago I prayed the prayer and asked God to be part of my life. I didn't want to say because I thought you'd laugh at me."

A wide grin spread across his face. "Now I'm even more certain, because that's another answer to prayer. I was worried about what you'd say."

I was happy – happy that Mark didn't want to leave me and even happier that we had both discovered a living faith and it was something we could share together. Somehow we'd been on a parallel track, unaware that we were both taking the same journey. But I still had concerns.

Later, as we sat cuddled together on the sofa and Mark opened the Bible that Andy had loaned him, he showed me some of the passages he'd been reading and told me how he'd become more and more certain that it was true. I leaned in against his firm shoulder and twisted the rough cotton cuff of his shirt between my fingers thoughtfully.

"What's up? Something's bothering you, isn't it?" His voice was gentle.

I moved away from him and hunched my knees together, wrapping my arms round them. My voice was a kind of whisper and filled with emotion. "I don't want you to change, Mark. I love you the way you are. You're a tough guy who nobody messes with and you're not afraid of a fight. I'm safe with you. I don't want you to become some soft wimpy Christian…" My voice trailed off and tears had begun to slide down my face.

Mark chuckled and pulled me toward him, laying the Bible to one side. "I'm still me, Brenda. I'll still look after you. I don't think God wants me to be a weed. I've just got to work it all out. Don't worry, I'm not letting you have one of my potatoes again – that was definitely a one-off!"

Chapter 6

September 1992: Werl, Germany

... a time to wait

Water gurgled and sloshed around the bottom of the bath as I bent over, rubbing vigorously with a sponge full of froth. My knees creaked as they pressed into the hard tiled floor and I reached for the showerhead to spray away the foam from the sides. I'd been cleaning the flat for the past hour – first the lounge and the kitchen and now the bathroom. I needed something to do, something to take my mind off this morning.

What's wrong with me? What if it never happens? What will Mark think? He might stop loving me... what if he leaves me? The muddled thoughts and fears were ringing round inside my head. I flushed the toilet and snatched up the little bin under the sink. Yanking out the plastic bag full of empty loo rolls and face wipes, I caught sight of the pregnancy test stick with its little window showing pink and blue markers. *Why did I even bother to do the test?* I should have known I was about to have my period – all the signs had been there, but I had just wanted to ignore them.

Mark and I had been married five years now and there was

still no baby. We hadn't been trying for very long – not years like some people, and I was only twenty-four. About a year earlier Mark had given me the shock of my life. He had come back off exercise and announced that it was time we tried to start a family. I was terrified. I didn't feel mature enough to have a baby and all the responsibility that entailed. The next month when my period came, I was relieved, and then the following month too. But after the fourth month, it didn't feel good any more.

I'd wondered what was wrong and rung my mum. She'd reminded me about the operation I'd had before I even met Mark. They'd discovered my womb was upside down and back to front and I'd had an operation when I was sixteen to put it right. The doctors had told me it might mean there would be problems conceiving. As a teenager without a boyfriend it hadn't bothered me much; all that had seemed a million miles away. I'd completely forgotten about it, until I'd spoken to my mum. Now, being married to Mark, it was different.

As the months passed, not being able to conceive began to feel more and more painful. People back home made it hard too, with their comments and questions about when we were going to start a family. Everyone joked about how time was ticking on, and my brother and his wife already had a child. Here on the quarter patch it was hard to get away from kids and babies. Even in the NAAFI (our local forces shop) or the med centre there was always someone waddling in heavily pregnant, usually with a few other sticky toddlers in tow.

I twisted the neck of the plastic bag and stepped into the hall to stuff it into the bulging black sack of kitchen waste that was waiting to be taken outside. A light tap at the door almost made me jump, and I stepped over the rubbish and pulled open the front door. Kathy was beaming at me as she stood on the doorstep, holding out a paper bag that smelt of freshly baked somethings.

"Treat time?" she said as she stepped in. "Oooh, smells of cleaning." As she walked through to the kitchen, she began telling me about how she'd nearly run over an elderly German lady in the town who'd stepped in front of her bike on the way to the bakery.

Sitting at the kitchen table sipping coffee and wiping the sugar from the doughnuts off my lips, I giggled. "We won't tell the blokes we've had doughnuts." She shook her head solemnly, still munching. "Or they'll try and get us doing extra time down on the weights!"

"Is Mark doing the Alpha Bible study tonight?" she asked.

I nodded mid-mouthful. A few months earlier Mark had bought the complete Alpha course, a group study all about God and the Christian faith, which he used when it was his turn to lead the home Bible studies on the "patch" – our nickname for army married quarters. He said it was easier for the lads to understand than a church service and allowed them to ask questions. It was all very exciting.

"Hopefully Ronnie and Anne will come," I said, and then I started giggling. "Let's hope he isn't in the same get-up as Sunday!" We both started laughing. Ronnie was also in Recce platoon and was a good friend of Mark and Andy's. He was taller than both of them, had a huge smile, and had recently married a lovely girl from Armagh. We were all delighted that he'd recently become a Christian.

When we had gone to our church the previous weekend, which was on an American airbase near Munster, the friendly welcomers told us they would be having baptisms during the service. I'd seen Ronnie chatting with one of the leaders and, as we took our seats, he leaned across and announced, "I'm going to be baptized!" Andy and Mark both clapped him on the back, telling him it was fantastic.

As the service progressed and the singing grew louder, someone came to lead Ronnie away to change for the baptism, which was to be a full immersion ducking in the portable pool which had been brought in. It was a bit larger than a hot tub, with steps up to it, and it had been set up in front of all the chairs. The musicians were playing rousing hymns, while the American pastor started talking and asking if anyone else wanted to come forward to be baptized.

The candidates, including Ronnie, emerged from a door at the side. We were all so happy that he was taking the important step of declaring his faith publicly, but when he walked out we could see he was wearing what looked like a blue and white choir gown, with a frill at the neck. It looked so out of keeping on his tall muscular frame, and certainly not what a soldier would want to be seen wearing. We all started giggling and bent our heads, trying to control ourselves and conceal our laughter. Ronnie certainly had a talent for making us smile. After the baptism, he was laughing about the gown too, and said it was all they had offered him because he hadn't come prepared with a change of clothes. He was on a high after the service and had taken it all in good spirits, but that get-up for the baptism was going to be a source of ribbing for many months to come, especially from Andy and Mark.

Kathy pushed the sugary plate away from her. "I shouldn't have eaten that really, but it's Friday, so practically the weekend…" She turned her mug around and grasped it in both hands, smiling across at me. At least Kathy and Andy weren't having children yet either – that helped a bit. Kathy was so quiet; she never intruded or asked questions. Usually it was me who did all the talking, only this morning I didn't feel like it. I wanted to confide in her about the negative pregnancy test and all my fears that we might not be able to have children. But then she'd probably say we should pray, and I didn't feel all that comfortable about praying for a baby. I thought if God wanted to give us one, it would just happen. *What if we're being punished for something?* I sipped my coffee and looked out of the window, forming a silent prayer in my head without much faith that it would change anything.

* * *

The huge chestnut trees along the road were beginning to drop their leaves, and golden, red, and yellow piles had started to form in heaps beside the pavement and next to the low hedges bordering the concrete houses and blocks of flats. I lowered the heavy shopping bags to the ground and rubbed my arms, wondering how, when I'd only popped out for some milk and potatoes, I had come back with two massive bags of food. Beyond the hedge I could hear children in the school playground screaming and shouting to one another, before a sharp whistle cut through the noise. There was a patter of shoes on tarmac as their morning break was cut short.

At the top of the stairs I eased the key into the latch and found I was still breathing heavily. *Why am I so exhausted? I've hardly done anything...*

In the kitchen I spooned some granules of coffee into a mug, but as I poured out the steaming water, the scent of the coffee made my stomach churn. I stood back from the smell and ran a glass of water instead. *What's the matter with me?*

Mark had been as calm as ever about the baby thing. I knew he wanted it as much as I did, but he had stroked my head when I had told him about the failed test a few weeks ago. "We've got to be patient, Brenda. It will happen at the right time."

I wished I had his quiet confidence. Mark wasn't due back till later that night because it was a Wednesday, and that meant sports afternoon in the army. He and Andy would be on the rugby pitch as ever. Even when they came home they'd probably go down to the cellar and lift weights. Mark was fanatical about his fitness. I suddenly felt weary and decided to put my feet up for five minutes before I tackled the latest pile of ironing.

A bird was squawking loudly, and in my dream there were hundreds of them. I was running through a wood that turned into a subway tunnel, and when I looked back there was a black cloud of giant birds following me. I stumbled and my stomach lurched as I fell to the ground. I woke with a start and a large rook took off with a flap of wings from its perch on the windowsill outside. I glanced at my watch and realized I'd been sleeping for a couple of hours. *But I never sleep in the day.*

I wandered into the bathroom and opened the cabinet. There was just one test stick left in the packet. I'd told myself not to use it until I was almost sure. Back in the kitchen I stared at the calendar on the wall. It had been six weeks since I'd done the last test.

* * *

"Mark? Mark, can you hear me?"

"Yer, I can hear you, Brenda."

"I tried to call earlier… but… when are you coming home?"

I could hear a babble of voices in the background, and then a raucous laugh and some jeering almost smothered the sound of his voice. "Err… not so long. Why? What's the matter?"

My heart was beating fast and my hand holding the test stick was shaking slightly. I knew I ought to wait until he was home, but somehow it wouldn't be real unless I told him. "I did a test, Mark… I'm pregnant. It says I'm pregnant: it's blue. We're going to have a baby!"

I was crying now, and I heard Mark whoop with joy. "That's incredible, Brenda – I'm going to be a father! Wait till I tell the boys!"

"Come home soon, Mark. I want to see you."

"Yer, that's fantastic! I'll be back as soon as I can, but I'm going to tell the lads now."

It was several hours before I heard the door click open. I'd left the pregnancy test out on the table. When he walked in, his arms were behind his back. I was trying to look cross, but I was still excited. "What took you so long, Mark? You've been hours."

He shook his head. "I know. I'm sorry. I was telling the lads and everyone was patting me on the back and wanted to buy me drinks… you know, they were all excited too that I'm going to be a father!" I was frowning. Then he stretched out his arms, with a bunch of flowers in one hand and a bottle of wine in the other.

"I bought you these to celebrate."

I couldn't help smiling as I stepped into his arms. His kiss smelt of beer and he wrapped his arms around me.

"I told you it would happen at the right time," he said. "God had it all in hand."

May 1993

I had never felt so enormous. I slid my legs to the edge of the bed and sat forward with my hands on my swollen belly. I was back in my old room with its blue and white floral curtains and navy carpet. It was as if time had stood still, and yet everything had changed. I stroked my bump through the stretched material of the light cotton shirt. It felt as tight as a drum and ready to pop. Now the time had come I was a little anxious about how it would all happen. The baby was breech, I'd been told a few months ago, and they had given me a date for a caesarean. It would be too dangerous to deliver the baby naturally, especially as I had been opened up before for a major operation. I looked across at my open hospital bag which had been packed and ready for the last few days. In a way, having a caesarean had made it easier for

Mark to book the time off, so all being well he would be there too. Our discussions a few months ago about me having the baby in Belfast seemed like a distant memory…

"I'm not giving birth here, Mark. I don't care if lots of other wives do. I want my mum around and I want the baby born in Northern Ireland."

I banged the iron down into the rack with a thud and Mark looked up at me with half a smile quivering on his lips. He was doing something with a piece of khaki twine which was spread out across his legs. "No need to get upset, Bren. I knew you'd want to be in Ireland. I was just checking."

He was laughing at me now and I realized he'd just been winding me up as usual to get a reaction, which I'd given him for the past five minutes. I'd ranted on about what I'd heard about clinical German hospital care, without food and no curtains round the beds. I picked up another rugby shirt and began shaking it out vigorously, wanting to be cross with him still, but I couldn't manage it for long. I looked down at the growing bump and stroked my tummy gently. *What does this little baby think about all the discussions?* Then, almost in answer, I felt a prod, as if someone had nudged me from the inside.

"He's kicking, Mark. I felt him kick me."

Mark laid aside his tangled twine and leaned his arms on the ironing board, looking intently at my tummy. "It might not be a boy, you know. What if it's a girl?"

I shook my head and said, "I've got a feeling it's a boy. Come and put your hand here, it might happen again."

He reached across, and as he laid his hand on my side, I felt the nudge again. A slow smile spread across his face. "Definitely got some strong limbs in there – boy or girl!"

"I hope you're going to be able to be there, Mark… I want you there. Do you think there's a chance?"

"There's definitely a chance if you go to hospital in Belfast...
and we need to put in for your flight back soon."

* * *

The car door banged shut and my brother glanced round at the
three of us crammed in the back seat. "Everyone ready? Have
you got everything, Brenda?"

"Come on, come on, Ian. We don't want to make her late." My
mum was glancing anxiously at her watch.

I was crushed in between my mum and my sister Gillian. My
sister-in-law, Isobel, was in the front passenger seat. Someone
was missing. "Where's Daddy?"

There was a communal sigh and I looked back as the car
pulled away. My father was standing alone on the doorstep. My
heart skipped a beat. I wanted him to come too, and I looked at
my mum. "What about Daddy?" I was craning my neck to look
back at him.

"He'll follow on – sure he'll probably be there almost as
quickly on the bus." She patted my hand. It all felt unreal, but I
was sad to leave my dad behind. I wanted him to be with us. Not
many girls would expect their father to come along for the birth
of the first grandchild, but my dad was always ahead of his time.
He'd even been there when my sister Gillian was born, in the
days when fathers didn't usually get involved.

* * *

I stared down at my arm swelling under the blood pressure band.
The nurse slowly let out the air and smiled at me. "All looks
normal," she said.

The door beyond swung open and Mark glanced around
before spotting us. He was dressed in jeans and a burgundy sweat
top, and his beautiful dark, wavy hair had been shorn in favour

71

of the standard army number one cut. I took a deep breath. He might as well have had "soldier" tattooed on his forehead – his height, his broad shoulders, and that booming English voice was a total giveaway. Even the colour of his top shouted, "Paras!" They were a regiment with a bad reputation in Northern Ireland, largely owing to their involvement in Bloody Sunday and the wounds from that event, which had been reopened very recently with the launch of an inquiry.

As he walked toward me I gave a weak smile, thinking, *I hope no one picks him out*. The dangers for the military in a local hospital were ever present and I knew he was vulnerable. He was currently living at Fort White Rock, a fortified base in West Belfast. Mark and his platoon would only go out with armoured vehicles to protect them, and they weren't usually allowed into civilian locations in case they were recognized by the IRA. But he had been given special permission to be there for the birth, and would be picked up afterward by a driver.

The next hour or so became a blur of dream-like memories. I could hear an old Sunday school song in my head as I faded in and out of consciousness, and I could see the smiling face of the anaesthetist as he hummed, "He made the stars that shine... He made the rolling seas..."

When I woke up, Mark was in a green gown beside me, and one of the nurses was handing me a bundle wrapped in a soft waffle blanket, which was pink. "Here's your daughter," she said. "She's beautiful."

"Daughter?"

I couldn't believe we had a baby girl. Then I began to shake and Mark took her from my arms as I went into shock from the operation. I must have fallen asleep or passed out because when I opened my eyes, I was on the ward again and Mark was sitting beside me. He stroked my cheek and told me I was amazing.

Then he gazed down at the perfect pink cheeks of the baby in his arms, touching her smudge of hair.

"She doesn't look like an Alexandra to me," he said. It was one of the girl's names we'd both agreed on. I reached out my arm, pushing down the blanket so that I could see her face properly. She was perfect. Everything was perfect, from her tiny nose and ears down to the miniature hands and fingernails. We decided on Victoria, but I was still getting my head around the fact that this wasn't a little boy. I'd even dreamt the night before that I'd had a baby and it was a boy.

I realized the morphine was making me sleepy, so I pushed it away and tried to hunch up the bed a little. I knew Mark would have to leave soon and I didn't know when I'd see him again. But I winced at the pain in my tummy.

"Stop your pain, Brenda," he said, urging me to take the morphine again. "I've got to go soon. They've said my lift has arrived."

He looked into my eyes, stood up, and laid the baby back in the plastic cot beside the bed. As he bent to kiss me, I could feel his cheeks were moist with tears and I began to cry too. I watched as his tall figure disappeared down the corridor and I heard the doors swing shut.

A few minutes later, as I blew my nose and wiped my eyes, the girl in the bed across from me called out in a broad Northern Irish accent, "Is that your husband?"

I nodded, too upset to speak.

"He's a soldier, isn't he, love?"

"No," I said. "No, he's not." I was terrified to admit I was married to a soldier.

"I know he is," she said.

I stayed silent then, scared for Mark and scared for us all, especially the little bundle sleeping beside me.

* * *

The next day I was able to sit up in bed. I had more conversations with the girl opposite and was a little less worried that she was a security threat. I realized she was only trying to be friendly. I put down the mug of tea on the bedside table and heard a bell echoing down the corridors of the ward. Seconds later a flood of visitors trooped in. Young fathers made their way to the bedsides of the other women around the bay and I watched jealously as they lay across the beds and picked up their newborns lovingly. *Why can't my husband be here?* I wished he would walk in and surprise me, but I knew it wouldn't happen. I picked up a magazine and tried not to look around at the obvious joy and special moments being soaked up by the couples at all the other beds. The next few days felt even worse, and as visiting hour dawned each afternoon, I drew the curtains around the bed so I didn't have to see what was going on. I felt so alone as I told myself, *I married a soldier. This was always going to be part of it.*

"He was the type of guy that you would always want next to you on patrol."

Major (now Colonel) Karl Hickman

CHAPTER 7

January 1994: Werl, Germany

... a time to embrace

A burst of baby laughter erupted from the pushchair ahead as Mark wiggled it from side to side, enjoying the simple delights of Tori's reaction. Although she had been christened Victoria, it wasn't long before we had shortened her name to Tori. I paused to watch them, wishing he wasn't leaving again so soon. The gravel path ahead was disappearing into a bank of fir trees, where the winter sunshine was filtering through in feathery stripes to the stones below. There were only a couple of hours of daylight left and I could feel the minutes ticking past like a time bomb – counting down the hours until his departure to the Special Forces selection course.

We were settled now. After months of separation we had at last begun to feel like a family. Caring for a new baby was exhausting, but since we'd come back to Germany and Mark had finished his tour, life had begun to slot into a routine. He was still putting in the long hours on fitness training, mainly in preparation for the course. It was what he wanted. I didn't want to stand in his way, but I felt uneasy about the future if he were to get through. Life was uncertain enough with postings, operational tours, and training. At least most of the time I knew where he was, even if I was worried. If he joined the SAS, I would never know where he was or what he was doing. *How would that feel?*

I drew in my coat more tightly. It was January and I could feel the temperature starting to drop.

The evening before, we'd finally managed to settle Tori after her bath and I was leaning against Mark on the sofa, sipping a glass of wine. "When did you decide you wanted to join the army?"

Mark stroked my hair. "I can hardly remember. I think I always did."

"How did you get the idea, though?"

He didn't answer immediately. "Grandpa. It must have been Grandpa. He and Uncle Gordon took me to an army parade in Salisbury. I remember watching the regiment marching past, all in line with their shiny boots and belts. I must have been about six. I thought I'd like to be a soldier. I was easily impressed. Still am," he added, with a grin.

I prodded him in the ribs. "Watch it!"

I knew Mark hadn't had an easy childhood, so perhaps joining the army had been a bit of an escape. His mum and dad had separated when he was very young and then his mum, Dianne, had met Roger. Mark remembered seeing his father occasionally, but when he was about eight, his dad was killed in a car accident. Mark was the eldest; he had a sister Joanne and a younger brother Kevin, both from Dianne's first marriage.

Soon after Dianne and Roger were married, his half-brother Darren was born. Mark obviously felt the responsibility of looking after his younger siblings and was fiercely protective of them, standing his ground in playground fights on their behalf.

From what I understood, there hadn't been a lot of money around in those days; he'd talked about pouring water on their breakfast cereal because there wasn't enough money to buy milk. Mark had tried to help by taking a weekend job in the local food shop.

When we were packing up his old room he showed me a poem he'd written at the age of fifteen – it was clever and funny. The heading at the top was "Physics Mock exam II". It was quite a long poem, with six verses.

1. Taking an exam which I'm certain to fail,
Sitting there silently in a private hall.
Looking around you see faces of frustration,
Pen and paper describe the fate of the nation.

4. Six months to go and I'll be all on my own,
Hopefully left school and far away from home.
But before I go I got a promise to keep,
That's to beat the system before they retreat.

He had also drawn a sketch of someone taking a punch at another figure on the back – all a sign of his frustration, I suppose. He didn't enjoy school and was keen to leave as soon as possible to join his local regiment – the Devonshire and Dorsets. It must have frustrated his teachers no end that he left after his sixteenth birthday in April, without even sitting his exams. He'd been due to take eleven O Levels. Despite all his potential, he had no qualifications when he joined up. He was so young he had to do an extra year of Junior Leaders' training. When he deployed to Northern Ireland on his first tour, he wasn't allowed out on patrol until the day of his eighteenth birthday.

* * *

Over the previous few weeks we had talked about the SAS selection process and what it would involve. I knew he would have pulled out if I'd asked him to, but I couldn't make him do that. I was proud of him. He was obviously doing so well and had sped through the ranks since I'd first met him. He was one of the youngest serving sergeants, and inspired respect in all around him. And although he now outranked Andy, their friendship remained strong. Everyone said he was a soldier destined for great things.

He'd been one of "Biles' Boys", as they were called, the favoured group of up and coming soldiers in the regiment. Major Chris Biles was his company commander in Berlin and now the Commanding Officer. Mark had introduced me to him at a party. Mark told me later that Chris had said, "You'd better marry her sooner than later if you want to hold on to her!"

I could see Mark excelled at his job, and it suited him so well. He was passionate about his fitness and yet he was also very serious about his drills and all the planning and admin. Andy reckoned Mark had a photographic memory, because he would just look at something they had to know and could virtually recite it word for word. He'd had experience with some covert operations already, as part of Recce Platoon, and had been involved in a close observation patrol in Northern Ireland on a previous tour. He'd told me about lying hidden behind a bush for days on end to keep an eye on a particular suspect, taking photographs, recording movements and meetings. He didn't mind roughing it – the hardest part for him had been missing out on his regular sessions in the gym while he was stuck in an observation post.

Once he had volunteered to gather vital information by watching a house where there was very little ground cover. He had come up with the plan to hide with others in a small, boggy pond in waterproof suits, surviving on only cold food for two days. The SAS guys in charge had been a bit concerned about the operation but had let it go ahead. Mark and the other two guys with him had survived without being "compromised" by the IRA, and the Special Branch had been supplied with the information they needed.

With all his talent and his ability to inspire and lead others, the Special Forces were an obvious next step. I could tell he was desperate to have a go and see if he could get in. The trouble was, I couldn't really see how he could fail, and that was scaring me.

"What happens if you get through, Mark? What happens to us?" I had asked him the previous evening.

He'd ruffled his hands through his hair. "I know it won't be easy, Bren, but if God wants me to get in, I will."

I couldn't argue with him, and inside I couldn't help hoping and praying that he wouldn't. When there didn't seem anything else to say, we'd prayed about it, asking God for the right outcome.

Now, as I increased my pace to catch up with them, I tried to let go of all the worries. I let out a deep sigh as I caught hold of his arm.

"Big sigh, Bren?" he said, looking down at me. I didn't need to say anything. He knew what was ahead. We both knew the score. More separation. More rushed, unsatisfactory phone calls and out-of-date letters. It was the way our relationship had started and seemed to be the way it was carrying on. Tomorrow he would steal out of the house at dawn and I'd hear his kit being bumped down the stairs. The calendar would come in to its own, with red crosses marking off the days until his return.

Tori gurgled happily, looking up at us and then staring above our heads at large birds flapping between the trees. I crushed his arm more tightly, wishing this wasn't another final day together.

"Are you cold?"

"I, err, a bit," I said.

He slid his arm around me. "When we get back, you could go on the stepper to warm up."

"Mark! Don't talk to me about the stepper today."

The exercise stepper machine had been Mark's present to me after Tori was born, and I had a love–hate relationship with it. I knew it was his way of encouraging me to get back in shape after the baby, and I wanted that too, but it was quite gruelling and a bit boring to work out on it. Also I didn't want to be told by him when to exercise, especially the night before he was leaving!

* * *

Bubbles from the bath were floating up in little clouds as I leaned forward to scrub my legs, before laying down again in the sweet-smelling water. I was quite pleased that my body was beginning to feel normal again, and while Mark was not around I was actually using the stepper more. The scales were less of a threat at the moment and I could see the pounds beginning to drop off. I was determined to be back to my old shape by the time he returned. I closed my eyes, enjoying the peace, knowing that Tori was at last fast asleep after a day of me chasing her round the flat, trying to have eyes in the back of my head while she pulled herself up on the furniture and crawled at high speed.

I wondered what Mark was doing now. Probably he was lying in a ditch somewhere with a bush on his head, or crawling through undergrowth in ice-cold conditions in the depths of the Welsh mountains. I knew he had done well the previous day. He'd sounded excited and full of confidence on the phone. He'd told me he had been well within his time on the Pen-y-fan run, so all seemed to be going well. I felt pleased for him and kept pushing away the underlying worries about the future.

I'd been praying more, too. We'd been looking at prayer in the Bible study group at the Padre's house, where Padre Simon Farmer and his wife Rachel had been encouraging a small group of us to explore new ways of praying. There seemed to be so much to learn. On the one hand we were told to ask for anything in His name and He would give it to us; on the other hand, we had to pray according to God's will. *How do I know what God's will is for us?*

I squeezed the sponge, watching the water and froth stream into the sea of bubbles below. The piercing bell of the telephone made me start. *Who could be ringing? Not Mark: he had only rung last night.* I hesitated, reluctant to leave the relaxing bath that felt like such a rare treat. The ringing continued. I leaned over and grabbed a towel, muttering under my breath, "Gillian, if it's you, I'm hanging up!"

Snatching up the receiver, I said, "Hello," and straight away heard Mark's voice on the line.

"Brenda, I'm coming back." He sounded flat and emotionless.

"What's happened?"

"I injured my knee on the run today. They say I might need an operation on it. I'm out."

I didn't know what to say. I could feel his dreams crumbling like a tower of cards. A bad fall was all it had taken to send the whole lot crashing down.

"Oh, Mark, I'm sorry. I'm so sorry, honey. It must be awful. I know what this meant to you."

He didn't say much, except that he would see me soon. His voice sounded wobbly, as if he was struggling to control his emotions. When I put the phone down I didn't feel like getting back in the bath. I knew he would be bitterly disappointed and I didn't know how he would react. I had wanted him to come home so much, but not like this.

* * *

It took Mark some time to get over the disappointment, and I was shocked to see how downhearted he looked when he hobbled in a few days later. I suppose he'd been keeping all his emotions locked in because when he held me, I could feel him start to sob. He was a great tough guy, but to be knocked out by an injury at this stage was hard to bear. I hadn't understood quite how much it had meant to him and how hard it was to go back and face everyone, knowing he hadn't made it.

When he sat down the tears continued to flow. All that effort and training seemed to be wasted. I started to tentatively mention the possibility of trying again, wanting to console him, but he just shook his head. That was it, as far as he was concerned. There was a fair bit of pride involved. He wouldn't be trying again. Later he talked to Andy on the phone, who was shocked to hear he was back and called him a "girl's blouse" for failing. I started to hear some of their usual banter and felt relieved that Mark sounded more like himself.

May 1995: Paderborn, Germany

I banged shut the boot of the car and turned to hook the changing bag on the back of the buggy. The battered old Mazda was in desperate need of a clean. But at least the mud hid the rust. Mark often joked that it was only the Christian fish symbol on the back of the car that was holding it together. Tori was kicking her feet against the step of the buggy and I was hoping she might be ready for a nap later, after a couple of hours in the crèche. Pushing the buggy up the straight path toward the church, I thought about being here a few days earlier with Mark, on our last Sunday together.

The goodbyes seemed to come around so frequently these days. It hardly seemed long since he had returned from Belfast, then disappeared on training to Canada, just before we'd all moved across Germany with the regiment to a new Garrison at Paderborn. Now he had gone again for the six-month UN peacekeeping tour to Bosnia. This time I planned to spend a couple of weeks in Germany and some time back in Ireland. It seemed like a good way to break up the separation. Tori was already asking for her daddy.

Inside the church the blue carpet up the aisle looked freshly hoovered and the light wood chairs smelt of polish. A group of wives were chatting beside a long table to the right of the door, where fresh bread and a board with cheeses were being arranged for lunch.

"Morning, Brenda," a voice from behind me said, with the slightest hint of an accent. A tall, well-built man with a thick mop of white hair and wire-rimmed glasses paused to look down at Tori and shake her hand.

"Hello, Carsten. Say 'hello', Tori," I said, squatting down to reassure her. I noticed the leather briefcase gripped in his left hand. "Are you off to a meeting next?" I asked, nodding at the case. "Or have you got some top-secret documents in there?"

Carsten's eyes lit up and he drew the briefcase toward him with both hands. "It's not a secret, but they are very valuable documents. I brought them to show everyone later. Can you think what they might be?"

Carsten Thiede was a clever man. He was a Lay Reader at the Garrison church in his spare time and married to an English woman called Fran. His main job was something to do with dating papyri and other ancient documents. He was a great academic and a specialist whom I often found hard to follow. He and Mark had many interesting discussions about the Bible's origins and the evidence of dates for when parts of the New Testament were written. Mark was in awe of his knowledge and was very excited when he realized Carsten had written one of the books he was reading on Matthew's Gospel.

"I haven't a clue, unless it's a bit of the Bible," I said in answer to his question, half laughing.

"You're right," he whispered. Then he tapped the briefcase gently with one hand, saying, "Inside here there are actual fragments of the book of Esther."

"Wow! Amazing..." I was impressed and eager to see what they looked like.

Today Carsten was leading our weekly lunchtime Bible study, which included a bread and cheese lunch. It was mainly attended by military wives, although occasionally some of the lads came if they could get away from work for an hour. Since Padre Simon had deployed with the regiment, Carsten was likely to be the only man in attendance for a few months. I was just about to ask how he'd come to be in possession of part of the original text of the Bible when everyone was summoned to collect their plate of bread and cheese, and there was no more time for questions.

I was grateful for the sense of camaraderie among the wives. We all had young children and so the studies were always punctuated by their noises as they played on the carpet below and requested drinks or more food. It was OK to ask questions and raise doubts at these sessions too. It never felt like anyone was looking down on me or thought I should know the answer or have more faith. Praying together helped. I felt strangely strengthened by the lunchtime session and more able to face the rest of the day.

A lot had happened since that Sunday when Mark and I had both confessed to being Christians. It hadn't been dramatic and we were still the same people. I still got mad with Mark and threw mugs across the kitchen when he wound me up. He was still the tough guy soldiers respected. But there had been a change in him, and people had noticed. Other soldiers in the platoon had also become Christians and the platoon had begun to have a reputation as "the God Squad". Mark told me that he and Andy were often asked questions about God and their faith, but they didn't shout about it or try to convert their mates. One day a soldier who'd been told Recce was a good platoon to join came up. He said he'd heard they were all Christians and didn't that mean they were "woofters"? Mark said, "If you want I'll take you round the back and beat you up, if it helps." I couldn't help smiling. Of course he wouldn't have really hurt the guy, but that was Mark's sense of humour. He was a man of few words.

Our good friends Andy and Kathy moved away, and Mark and I both missed them. They left a huge gap after Andy left the army for the second time and they went to live in Australia. We promised to visit once we'd saved up for the airfares. Alongside Andy and Kathy, we had been part of a close-knit group of friends who had met for Bible studies each week, but most of them had been posted away over the last year. Constant change and saying farewell to good friends was part of army life. I'd made new friends through the church, and with each new challenge and disturbance I was becoming better at adapting and finding my feet again. The main thing was that although Mark went away, he always came back. He was the solid point, the rock in my life, and the centre around which I found my bearings.

"He had that air of self-confidence, born of quality,
which the very finest soldiers have."

Lieutenant Colonel (now Major General)
Rupert Jones

CHAPTER 8

December 1996: Plymouth

... a time to learn

Christmas had arrived. The turkey was already roasting and Mark was heating up some mulled wine as a reward for peeling the vegetables. Spicy and alcoholic aromas were drifting through from the kitchen, reminding me of a German Christmas market. I squatted down beside the bauble-laden tree in the window and breathed in the scent of fresh pine needles. Brightly wrapped parcels in all shapes and sizes were in disarray around the base of the tree, since Tori had hauled out her largest present, which she had ripped open breathlessly. I leaned forward to reach some of the smaller gifts that had almost disappeared underneath the branches.

Tori was singing softly and rocking the bright red Teletubby doll in her arms. "Go to sleep, little Teletubby. Go to sleep, little Po... go to sleep, my baby."

The precious toy had been on her Christmas list for several weeks and so it was a shock when we'd gone out to buy one and discovered they were all sold out. After ringing round frantically, we'd eventually found a shop that had one, and Mark's sister, Joanne, had managed to find it and deliver it just in time. Tori glanced up at me and put her finger to her lips to stop me from speaking. "He's sleeping, Mummy, and I'm going to put him in the pushchair now... you have to be quiet!"

"OK," I said with half a smile. I couldn't think where she had seen all this childcare – probably at nursery. *She'd love a little brother or sister... one day.*

Mark appeared in the doorway, clapped his hands, and then rubbed them together. "That's the vegetables all done. We can open some more presents soon!"

"Sshh..." we both responded. "The baby's sleeping!" I hissed, pointing at the strange red toy with an odd-shaped hat on its head.

Mark raised his eyebrows and opened his eyes wide in mock surprise, fighting back a smile. Looking at Tori, he whispered, "If we're very quiet opening the presents, do you think it will be OK? I really want to open one of mine."

Tori looked up at him and smiled, then she laid the sleeping Teletubby down on a cushion next to her and patted it. "He'll be fine," she said, and she trotted toward the pile of presents. "Are there any more for me?"

We both squatted beside her. "I'll see if we can find one," I said, reaching for a very small box which I knew was from her auntie. I helped her peel back some of the wrapping and she squealed with delight at the little plastic shell which opened up to reveal a tiny sitting-room with tiny people in it.

"It's a Polly Pocket, Tori. How lovely. Isn't Auntie Gillian clever? I wonder how she knew you wanted one." Tori picked up the tiny person in her finely painted dress and shoes and turned her round in her fingers, enchanted by the detail of the miniature toy.

Several other presents were unwrapped between us. Mark slid on the new jumper I'd bought him and grinned at me, pushing out his chest. I reached in and pulled out a small package about the size of a book. The label said, "My Darling Brenny, now it begins", which was puzzling. I ripped open the parcel and saw it was a book – *Roget's Thesaurus*.

I looked up at Mark. "Err, thanks."

He was smiling. "You'll be needing it, Brenda." Then he reached over and handed me another small parcel from the base of the tree. "And this."

"Another book?" I was trying not to sound ungrateful. But perfume or some nice clothes would have been more along the lines of what I'd been hoping for. I tore away the wrapping to reveal an Oxford dictionary with a folded sheet of paper on top. It was the receipt for a payment with the Open University logo at the top.

"What's this?"

He moved across to sit beside me on the floor. Tori paused in her play to watch us.

"I've paid for your first course on an Open University degree."

"What?!" I was astounded. I had never in a million years expected him to get me something like that. I kissed him and thanked him and he slid his arm round me. "It's to make up for you giving up doing a degree when we got married. You're clever, Brenda, and I always promised you'd go to university in England."

It would mean a lot of work, and by the look of the cost of the first part, it would also be very expensive. But this was a way for me to become qualified and get a job that demanded more skill than wiping bottoms and cleaning up vomit. As the realization of what it meant sank in, I put my arms around his neck and kissed him. "I love you, Mark Hale. Who else would buy their wife a dictionary for Christmas?"

1998

A smell of stale cigarettes and damp carpet hit me as I opened the door, and I went straight to the window to let in some fresh air. There had been a big dinner the previous evening and debris from the young officers' antics lay all around the corridors of the Mess. I pulled the sheets off the bed and stripped off the pillowcases. Wedging open the door, I dropped the dirty linen into a large blue bag and began to drag the hoover into the room. Coffee or something like it had been spilt down a wall beside the sink in the corner, leaving a dark stain on the burgundy carpet below. I sighed. *Better get on with it. This is paying for our next OU modules.* We definitely needed the money. Tori was going to private nursery now and Mark had also started an OU degree in psychology. It was all more than we could afford on just one salary.

Mark hadn't been too sure about me taking the cleaning job in the Officers' Mess. "What about Tori?" he'd asked. "Who will look after her while you're cleaning?"

"She'll be at nursery those mornings. It's all OK. If they want me other days, I can always ask a friend to have her for a couple of hours. She'll be fine."

He shook his head and I could tell there was something else bothering him. He was bending down to adjust the chain on the rower in the garage and I leaned back against the wall, watching him. I wasn't going to give up just because he didn't like his wife being a cleaner. "We need the money, Mark, especially with you starting your course soon."

He turned toward me. "You can't trust the young officers, Brenda. Some of them have got no scruples. They'll try it on with anyone and they don't care if the girls are married. You're very attractive. I don't want them taking advantage of you while you're cleaning their bedrooms."

I laughed. "I can look after myself, Mark. I won't let them mess with me. I'll tell them who I'm married to and that will scare them!"

He flashed me a warning look. "It would be better if you found something else."

But I hadn't, and in the end it had worked out fine. I enjoyed the banter with some of the young officers I bumped into occasionally. A few of them knew Mark, and they seemed to treat me with more respect once they knew I was Colour Sergeant Hale's wife. Some of them joked about Mark's obsession with fitness and told me about him building a "field gym" while they were out in Bosnia. I'd only heard snippets about the last tour, and communication hadn't been easy while they were moving all over the place during their operation. I discovered Mark had led the charge to create a gym, and his old mate Alan Foot, whom we all called Sox, told me that Mark had convinced him and other members of Recce platoon to pack less kit so that he could get his weights out on the operation. Some were even stored inside their Scimitar vehicles. When the opportunity came while they were field based for a few weeks, Mark directed tasks for building the field gym in a small clearing, setting up pull-up bars in the trees and improvised workout areas, using his weights and other items to create an exercise programme. It didn't surprise me – he was never happy unless he could keep up his fitness. Apparently Mark and a few others would spend hours in the "gym" in between training and other tasks.

When I'd heard Mark talk about the tour, he'd mentioned some hairy moments, which included deliberately having to get themselves arrested by testing checkpoints and driving through at speed or avoiding being shot by the locals, all while they travelled around without any weapons to protect themselves. When the regiment's role changed mid-tour from a UN peacekeeping force to a rapid reaction force, called Task Force Alpha, the vehicles all had to be repainted from white to green, signifying their changed mandate. Mark decided to add an Ichthus fish, the secret early Christian symbol, to each of the vehicles, and no one seemed to bat an eyelid.

There were quite a few Christians in the platoon, and Mark led regular Bible studies throughout the tour, along with support from Padre Simon, who met with them regularly to lead services and pray with them. On the evening before they were due to leave to spearhead the planned push into Sarajevo to break the stranglehold the Serbs had over the Muslim population, Mark organized a final meal for the whole platoon. They all knew the platoon's chances of survival in the Scimitars were low, because they didn't have the protection of the armoured Warrior vehicles driven by the rest of the regiment. He said the final time together chatting and eating had felt a bit like the Last Supper. They'd all realized how serious the situation was when the war correspondents arrived, including the BBC's Kate Adie.

In the end, a few minutes before "H hour" when the operation was due to begin, it was stopped after the politicians realized the casualty rate would be far higher than first predicted. All the vehicles had been revving up to go, moments before they were due to leave, when the radio crackled, "Stop, stop, stop!" The task force was pulled back from the brink, and when they did eventually come off Mount Igman sometime later, they didn't have to fire a shot and drove into Sarajevo unchallenged by the Serbs.

As I swilled water around the sink I almost started laughing, thinking about Mark worrying over the risks of my job here in the Mess. It wasn't exactly dangerous compared to his antics on operations. But he always looked out for me, and now there was Tori to care for too. He was fiercely protective, and it felt good to know he always had my back.

* * *

I inched the skirt further toward my knees and glanced down at my black court shoes to check there was no mud on the heels. The navy blue chairs reminded me of a doctor's waiting room, but there were fewer of them and there was no coffee table with out-of-date magazines in the centre of the room. I glanced up at the large black and white clock on the wall above the desk and saw the hand move fractionally toward the hour. We were early. Mark was looking smart in his darkest jeans and a dark blue shirt. His lightweight jacket lay in a bundle on the chair beside him. He was resting his arms on his thighs, leaning slightly forward, and he glanced back at me and made a face. I giggled. "Bet you were always outside the headmaster's office," I said in a half whisper, hoping the PA at the desk couldn't hear me.

"Yer, but it wasn't as posh as this, and no coffee machine in the corner. We had to stand in the corridor so everyone saw us and knew who was in trouble. I suppose you never got sent to the head, Mrs Goody Two Shoes?"

I shook my head. "I'd have been terrified... still am."

We'd had a tour of the school already and were both very impressed. This, we hoped, would be Tori's first school. We so wanted a good place for her. Both of us were keen that it would be a Christian school with a strong ethos, and the only one we could find locally was this Roman Catholic school. St George's School had a good reputation and excellent results. The only problem was that neither Mark nor I were Roman Catholic. Mark's background was Jewish and mine was Northern Irish Presbyterian – we couldn't find a Catholic in our families since before the Reformation! Luckily the school had to admit fifty per cent of its children from the other Christian denominations. The application process had been long and drawn out and we'd had to ask the Padre to supply a letter to say that we were regular churchgoers. That wasn't a problem, but I was worried about what this interview with the head teacher might involve. *Will we be up to the mark? Are we the kind of parents he wants to have supporting the school?*

The door opened and a stocky man in a dark brown suit with neatly cropped grey hair stepped forward. "Mr and Mrs Hale?"

We stood up and he reached out his hand.

As we perched on the upright chairs in his office, he returned to sit behind his desk and leaned toward us. He had a friendly smile and seemed to want to put us at ease. "What's made you want to choose our school for your daughter?"

I glanced at Mark to see if he wanted to speak, but he nodded at me. I launched into our desire to have Tori educated in a Christian environment, with strong Christian values at its heart. He asked us about our own beliefs and we both told him how we had become Christians and what it meant to us now. He seemed happy with all our answers and there was time for us to ask questions at the end. As he led us to the door he said, "It's not our usual policy to inform parents immediately, but I want you to know that we would be happy to accept Tori, and we'll be sending through a letter to confirm her place."

We couldn't stop smiling, and as we turned the corner into the car park I did a little jig. "She's in, Mark… he said she's in!"

* * *

The playground looked smaller than I'd remembered, probably because it was buzzing with children and parents today. There were white painted circles and lines all across the tarmac surface, offering a range of games and activities from netball to hoop-throwing. Tori's hand was gripping mine tightly and I could feel a knot tightening in my chest as I wondered how she would feel going into this strange building without friends and following a complete stranger. Dressed in the winter uniform of grey skirt and socks and green jumper over a checked shirt, she was carrying a little cloth bag with her gym kit. I had painstakingly labelled her little shorts and T-shirt the previous evening, with tapes which had "Victoria Hale" printed on them in blue.

A bell rang and older children began to line up in front of the red double doors in the centre of the building. A clutch of other children, obviously starting for the first time too, hung back with their parents. I bent down and said, "Tori, sweetheart, it's time to go in. Shall we find your new class?"

She clung to my leg and started to whimper. Some of the other children were crying too as we moved toward the diminishing crowd. A woman with dark brown hair cut into a sharp bob appeared from another doorway and strode toward us, her hair bouncing from side to side. She was wearing a dark green dress with a short black jacket over the top, and the briefest of smiles flickered across her face. "What's all this?" she said, looking at Tori and another little girl who was also weeping. Then she took a hand from each of them and said, "Stop that noise at once and come along with me. We're going to find your teacher."

They were so surprised they didn't argue. As I watched them disappear into the building, I felt tears streaming down my own cheeks.

A few days later I watched Tori file into the same building chatting to another little girl and turning to wave and smile instead of cry. I pulled open the car door feeling ten times lighter, and noticed her pink lunchbox on the floor behind me. I sighed, reached over to pick it up, and relocked the car. Inside the school, the receptionist smiled and said it would be fine for me to take the forgotten lunchbox down to Tori's classroom. The corridor was quiet, and when I got to her class, I peeped in through the window in the door. I could hear her teacher's lilting voice. Mrs

Spanswick reminded me of Mary Poppins, sitting in an old-fashioned wing-backed chair, leaning forward with an open book on her lap and her pencil in her hand. All the children, who were dressed in varying shades of green or grey jumpers, were sitting on a carpet around her with their legs crossed.

"Yoo hoo! Tori!" She was waving at her and smiling. Tori raised her arm and said, "Here."

It was a very different way of taking the register, but very lovely.

I knocked gently and opened the door, waving the lunchbox. The class teacher smiled and nodded, then turned to continue with the register. As I made my way out to the car, I silently thanked God for the teacher and the school, and for Tori having such a fantastic start to school life.

* * *

I was relieved to see that the car park beside the library had spaces, and I snatched up the notepad with the list of books from the seat beside me. Tori might be learning her numbers and starting to read, but I had new studies of my own as well. It wasn't easy juggling a part-time job, mummy duties, cleaning, and washing, and then trying to squeeze in some reading and essay planning at the same time. The good thing was I found my degree in Social Policy fascinating. I liked the fact that I could go in the directions I was interested in and explore subjects like criminal justice.

Inside, the library had that distinctive book smell mixed with a hint of furniture wax. The two long tables were gleaming from the light through the windows. Searching the shelves by subject, I found a couple of useful books and then settled down at one end of an empty table and began to fill out an order form for some titles that were on my essential reading list. The rustle of newspaper made me glance up as an elderly man with a bald head and a green and orange scarf wound round his neck shook out his newspaper before settling back into the comfy chair beside a low shelf of CDs. As I stared at the regimental colours of his scarf, I thought, *I wonder if he's ex-D&D?* He lowered his paper slightly and caught my eye, almost as if he'd been aware I was staring at him. I turned back to my form, feeling a flush rise up my cheeks.

The scarf had made me think how proud Mark was of his orange and green D&D tie. Those two colours were now imprinted on my mind as a symbol of the regiment which he was so proud to serve in, with its motto *Semper Fidelis* – "always faithful". He was Wiltshire born and Dorset bred and proud to be English. That national arrogance had got him into trouble at times, particularly during his time in Berlin. Andy and Mark, along with other culprits from their platoon, had loved to fight. He'd told me about jumping on the roofs of cars and fighting with a gang of Turks before being chased by the German police and getting arrested on the U-Bahn underground. Once, he and Andy had been put in the guardroom after a boozy night out had turned into a brawl. Their punishment the next day was to run round the parade ground carrying a huge log painted orange and green. But Mark and Andy were so fit that it was impossible for the sergeant "beasting" them to wear them out.

I shifted the book I was looking at and tried to refocus on the words. It was a struggle at times, but Mark was studying too now and had begun his own OU degree in Psychology. He put me to shame, coming back from a day at work and then pulling his books out to absorb some complex theory. He was clever, and I felt that he was brighter than me, even though I was the one with the A Levels.

CHAPTER 9

September 2000: Twickenham

... a time to be born

"Craig is in the kitchen…" The Geordie narrator's voice made everything sound commonplace. But this was not an ordinary day in the *Big Brother* house. I leaned forward, eager to see what was going to happen next and who was going to be the first winner of this TV reality show which had gripped the nation.

I could hear Mark setting down a large bag in the hallway outside. "Come on, Mark, you're missing it," I called out.

He sank down on the settee and slid his arm around my shoulders. I nestled in against him, my heart fluttering slightly as I realized this would be the last time I would feel him next to me for another few months.

He shook his head. "I can't believe they've done this – made a programme out of people sleeping and cooking their tea."

The image changed from the kitchen to the crowd gathered outside the house, then to Davina McCall shouting into a microphone. It was so drawn out that we were both getting bored. I turned the sound down and snuggled in closer to his chest. *I should be used to this by now,* I thought. But tonight I felt terrible and my voice faltered as I said, "What time do you have to be there?"

I felt his hand stroking my hair. "I'll leave about eleven. We've got another hour yet."

An hour. Is that all? My heart was pounding and a lump was forming in my throat. He was off to Northern Ireland with the regiment for a six-month tour, which meant leaving his time on public duties at Windsor and going back out on the streets. He was now Sergeant Major of "A" company, with more responsibility.

We liked living in London, and life had improved considerably since I had managed to get a job in Tori's new school as a teaching assistant. Mark loved being in Twickenham too – the home of English rugby. We were living almost opposite the ground; some days we could even hear the roar of the crowd from the flat. I wove my fingers through his, tightening my grip. I really didn't want him to leave tonight, but I knew it was pointless saying anything. Silent tears started to slide down my cheeks and the images on the screen began to blur. Mark turned up the volume and we watched the last figure exit the house to screams and cheers. Craig Phillips was the winner and we both laughed as the Liverpool bricklayer received his crown, having won overwhelming public support during his stint on the programme.

I didn't usually cry until Mark had left the house and I didn't want him to see how upset I was this time, so I pressed my face against his chest, but somehow I couldn't stop sobbing.

"Hey, I'll phone tomorrow when I'm there. It's going to be fine, Brenda. I'll be back before you know it and getting under your feet again."

I looked up at him, smiling through my tears. "I don't know why it feels so bad this time, Mark," I said, brushing away the tears from my face and clearing my throat. "Shall I make us a cup of tea?"

I was trying not to make it even harder for him to leave. I kept telling myself I should be used to him going away and all the uncertainty of what might happen, yet rather than my fears getting less, it felt as if each time he deployed for months away, it was becoming harder.

* * *

The queue was moving slowly toward the entrance of the giant body we were about to enter. Alison was holding Tori's hand, and Tori's eyes were wide with wonder as she gazed up at the massive structure above us. We'd decided to visit the Millennium Dome before it was too late and the exhibition ended. My sister Alison had come to stay, which seemed like a good time to make the trip. It meant a lot of walking but Tori was old enough to manage, and because it was full of informative exhibits it seemed a fun way to have an educational day out. As we entered the pink tunnel, we could see the multicoloured tiles that made up the giant body in shades of pink, orange, and flesh tones. Tori held out an arm and ran her hand along the walls. It was a strange sensation when I reached out my hand too. The surface, which shone like ceramic tiles, turned out to be more rubbery than I had expected, with constantly changing shapes moving across it. The pace through the exhibition was slow and I took a swig from a bottle of water, feeling slightly lightheaded.

The first room was an exhibition on skin with giant hairs, a pierced belly button, and some ugly-looking bugs in display areas. My stomach was starting to churn. In the next room a spoof doctor tried to analyze Alison's skin, but she snatched her arm away and another volunteer stepped in. Next stop were the eyebrows. I was keen to move through the body as quickly as possible, hoping I wasn't actually going to be sick, but Tori was fascinated by the larger than life exhibits and asked a string of questions, especially when we got to the fertilization area of the body.

When we eventually emerged from the tunnels and escalators, I headed straight for a bench and sat down, taking deep breaths and more swigs of water.

"What's the matter, Brenda? Are you OK?"

I shook my head. "I don't know. I just felt awful – really sick. Maybe I was getting claustrophobic."

Alison perched on the seat beside me and patted her tummy, which was just beginning to show a slight bulge. "I thought I was meant to be the delicate one! Did you eat something odd this morning?"

I couldn't think why I felt so strange. We'd had a Chinese take away the previous evening and I was wondering if that was the cause. Tori leaned against my legs and unfolded the map of the exhibition. "Look, Mummy, we are here. There's a play area over there and this one says 'rest' if you want to go and lie down!"

We all laughed. "Just give me a few minutes, sweetie. I'll be fine soon."

Standing in a food queue a few minutes later, Alison whispered in my ear, "You're not pregnant, are you?"

Pregnant? Unlikely. I wanted to have another baby, but sadly it hadn't happened. I found the thought quite painful as I remembered the previous Christmas and the terrible realization that I was having a miscarriage. The loss had been all the more tragic as I watched Tori playing with her toys. I knew she would have loved a little brother or sister to join in. *I'm probably just run down*, I thought. I didn't even want to let myself hope.

* * *

Alison slid a paper bag across the table toward me. "Why not check? What harm can it do?"

"When did you get that?" I snapped.

She shrugged. "When I popped out for the paper. I thought it might be a good idea."

Tori was engrossed in cutting out figures from a magazine and sticking them into a large scrapbook which Alison had bought for her. I picked up the packet and walked to the bathroom.

Staring into the mirror, I pushed my fingers across my pale cheeks and then glanced down at the white test stick on the edge of the sink. *Wouldn't it be typical if I found out I was pregnant while Mark was away again?*

Five minutes later I emerged from the bathroom feeling dazed. Alison looked up and a slow smile spread across her face, then she rushed over and threw her arms around me. "I told you, Brenda. I knew you were."

Tori was watching us from the other side of the room. "What did you know, Auntie Alison?"

May 2001

Her tiny hands were just visible beyond the sleeves of the Babygro. She was perfect. This was our second daughter and we had called her Alexandra. I had thought she might be a boy for Mark, but he was overjoyed with his two girls. I sighed and then winced as I felt a tug on the stitches. I'd wanted to have a natural birth at home. When I told the doctors, they'd looked at my medical history, shaken their heads, and advised a hospital birth. A home birth was possible, they said, but I'd have to sign a disclaimer in case anything went wrong.

"You're not signing any disclaimer, Brenda. If the doctors say it's risky, we're not doing it. You'll have a caesarean in the hospital," Mark had told me. There was no messing about with

Mark; he wasn't prepared to take risks with my health or the health of our child.

This time around he had been able to book the morning off work. He had packed up the car and fixed in the new baby seat. We'd dropped Tori off with friends and driven straight to West Middlesex Hospital. Even though he had missed most of my pregnancy, I felt lucky that at least this time he was taking me in and would be there all the way through.

A few weeks earlier, I'd worried that he wouldn't be in a fit state if the baby were to come early. He had joined in the high jinks for the annual Army and Navy rugby match at Twickenham, which we could have almost watched from our flat. I'd heard the cheers and shouts during the afternoon and would have been there myself if I hadn't been about to give birth. Mark had dressed up as a sailor, but emblazoned across his navy and white hat was "ARMY" in huge letters. It was a sure way to wind up the Navy. After disappearing for a few drinks at the local pub where he met up with other regimental buddies, he rolled in just before lunch and said he wouldn't be late home after the match.

"Don't worry, Brenny, I'm not having any more."

If I'd believed that I'd have been an idiot. I knew he wasn't a big drinker, but he had to let his hair down occasionally. On this occasion it would have been better if he was sober enough to take me to hospital, just in case. I don't even know what time it was when he came in, but the next day he was suffering. I didn't have much sympathy.

We had made it anyway and without any dramas this time. I closed my eyes, picturing his face as he held our newborn daughter and cut the cord. He had been brimming over with pride and joy at the miracle of our second child.

* * *

"Mummy!"

An excited voice roused me. Tori was standing next to me and peering into the clear Perspex cot beside the bed. She was holding a pale pink bunny, which still had its label on. Her blonde curls bobbed excitedly and she was breathing quickly as if she'd been running. She held out the bunny for me to inspect. "Daddy said we needed to buy a present, so I chose this."

"It's gorgeous, Tori." I caught Mark's eye and he winked at me.

"We called at Mothercare, that's why we were a bit longer." He reached in and gently stroked the baby's cheeks. She sneezed suddenly and her arms flew up slightly before resting either side of her head.

Tori laughed and leaned in toward the cot. "Alexandra, Alexandra," she half whispered, "this is your bunny." She placed it gently on the side of the cot and let out a sigh. She wriggled next to me onto the edge of the bed. "When will you be coming home? Tomorrow?"

"Maybe. I hope so."

I was looking forward to going home, to having our family all together. There was a sense of completeness as I looked across at Mark holding baby Alexandra in his arms, while Tori leaned against him and stroked her hair. I thanked God silently for answering our prayers and remembered a verse from Ephesians I had read a few days ago: "Now to him who is able to do immeasurably more than all we ask or imagine, according to his power that is at work within us.' God really had done more than I could ever ask or imagine. I had a husband I loved so deeply and now we had two beautiful, healthy children. I was blessed.

"Hard to his core, he was immensely fit, strong and competitive, not least on the rugby field, where his gentle manner was discarded."

Lieutenant Colonel (now Major General) Rupert Jones

CHAPTER 10

September 2001: Twickenham

... a time to fight

The echo of boots on tarmac and rhythmic drumming signalled the arrival of the troops. I jigged the buggy gently, hoping Alix would stay asleep. We were among the select gathering of military dependants who had been given permission to watch the Changing of the Guard today. We had a privileged view of the ceremony from inside the gates, and I stood beside Mark's parents and Annabel Cleave, one of the officers' wives. Out in front of Buckingham Palace the Duke of York and the American ambassador stood rigidly side by side, ready to salute the Guard as they marched forward. The atmosphere was deeply solemn, and beyond the Palace railings I could see the flutter of hundreds of Stars and Stripes flags. The world was still reeling from the horror of what had happened in America just two days earlier at the World Trade Center. It seemed as if thousands of Americans had come to express their collective grief and to mourn together.

We were all still coming to terms with the terrible events that had taken place on 11 September. I could still picture the images in my head as I gazed out at the sea of faces beyond.

I had still been on maternity leave that Tuesday, and determined to get on the stepper for half an hour or so while Tori was at school. It was harder to shift the weight the second time around, but the stepper had done the trick before. The television news was on and I was gripping the stepper bar with one hand and pushing the buggy backward and forward with the other, attempting to rock the baby to sleep while I worked out.

Surreal images of a plane colliding with a skyscraper appeared, and I wondered what had happened to the news. It seemed as if the channel had changed on to a feature film. I reached across for the remote just as the news presenters appeared again. I couldn't take it in and increased the volume. My legs stopped moving as I stared at the screen. The newsreaders seemed to be struggling to take it in as much as the rest of us. Suddenly I needed to be with someone; I didn't want to watch this terrible news alone. I scooped up a dozing Alix and went down to the flat below.

My friend Shelly opened the door and I said, "Are you watching this?" She looked stunned and we sat down together, staring at the television. I thought about all the people we knew and how they might be affected. Tori's best friend at school was called Rhea and her father was an airline pilot. We both wondered what it all meant.

Later that day, as I moved around the flat, with the television offering people's reactions and continually rerunning the footage of the collapse of both towers, I began to wish we didn't live in London. *What if the same terror was played out here?*

When Mark arrived back I jumped up from the sofa. "What on earth is going on, Mark?"

His eyes slid across to the images on the news and his voice sounded flat and mechanical as he said, "London is on full alert. We need to be vigilant."

We both felt subdued as we ate our meal with images of people running from a cloud of dust filling the screen. He laid his knife and fork together on the empty plate, still gazing at the television, and then he said, "It's a game changer. This will change everything."

* * *

As the guard drew nearer, Tori squeezed my hand. She didn't say anything; she seemed to understand the seriousness of the situation. We all turned to watch the soldiers march onto the square. We'd only just made it from Twickenham to the Palace in time. I'd been running through Green Park, with Alix giggling in her buggy and Tori trying to keep up, while I took out anybody's ankles who didn't move quickly enough for us to pass. As the band and the guards moved ahead, I spotted Mark at the front, with his shoulders back.

He had an important role to play as the Company Sergeant Major and I knew this would be a very proud moment for him. The Devon and Dorsets were very distinguished in their blue uniform with peaked caps and white belts. Mark had a red sash across his jacket and took up position on the far left, standing rigidly with his rifle against his shoulder, while the band continued to play behind. Then as they moved into the American national anthem, I felt the goosebumps rise on my arms and a lump formed in my throat. At first there was a hushed silence, and then slowly those watching beyond the railings and waving forlorn flags began to join in with the words. I could see some of them placing their hands over their hearts and others wiping away tears. As the anthem reached its climax, the words were echoing out across the courtyard and round the surrounding park. Even the traffic outside seemed to have come to a halt.

When the music faded, there was a clatter of applause and the surrounding onlookers fell silent. I looked across at Mark who was staring straight ahead, his eyes shaded by the peak of his cap and his white-gloved hand clenched by his side. On our left a film crew were scanning the frozen parade. It was a break with protocol for another country's anthem to be played at the Changing of the Guard, but we'd heard that the Queen had given special permission for her troops to play the "Star-Spangled Banner" in tribute to the many who had died. When the silence ended and the salutes had been taken, the band played a selection of sombre American music. It was good to feel that we were standing "shoulder to shoulder with our American brothers and sisters", as Prime Minister Tony Blair had put it.

On the minibus going home, I gazed out at the familiar hum of London traffic, where browsing shoppers and tourists mixed with striding professionals in suits. I thought about all those who had lost someone they loved and who would be looking at the world very differently today.

A few days later, we heard that Tori's previous class teacher, who had moved to America during the summer with her husband's job, was among those grieving. He was one of the thousands who lost their lives when the twin towers collapsed. Somehow, knowing someone affected brought the tragedy closer, and as work hours and commitments increased for Mark, I often comforted myself with the thought that he and all those in the military, the police, and the security services were working to protect us from another 9/11.

* * *

Tori was skipping along the touchline beside me as I pushed the buggy over the grass. I was trying to catch sight of where the ball had gone. "Come on Daddy! Come on the Harlequins!" she shouted, clapping her mittened hands together and then waving her arms. We were faithful cheerleaders, the Hale girls, always on the touchlines cheering Mark on, whether it was army rugby or his latest foray into league games. Thankfully Alix was asleep, despite all the noise and the cold winter air.

The team had just come back on after half-time and I suddenly had a sense that something was wrong. Mark wasn't quite his normal self. He was one of the largest and toughest in the team and that made him a target. The other side were trying to take him out or rile him because he was "dangerous". I squatted down to tuck the covers further round Alix and caught sight of Mark not far away on the right of the pitch. I noticed a player from the opposite team approach him, and I gasped when I saw this player start to punch Mark. It wasn't playful: he was landing big solid punches into Mark's side. I could see Mark saying something and I heard him shouting for the referee, but the ball was in play on the far side of the pitch and he didn't hear.

The punching carried on and Mark grabbed the guy by the throat. I could see he was shouting "Stop!" but the player wasn't stopping: the player was laughing and lashing out. The next moment, Mark headbutted him and he went down on the ground. The whistle blew and the ref appeared. Players thronged around the guy on the ground and Mark stepped back. One of his team was chatting to Mark and nodding, and there was a brief exchange with the referee. Eventually the injured player staggered off and the match continued. I was thinking, *You got what you deserved, mate – that will teach you to mess with my Mark!*

Rugby had been a part of our lives for years, ever since Andy Moreland had got Mark into it not long after we were married. Although Mark had only recently started to play for the Harlequins' second team he had been a kingpin of battalion and army rugby, usually playing flanker. He was supremely fit and he was a big guy, so rugby suited him. Over the years the regimental team had become like family and I was somehow part of it. He would go out on their raucous nights out and I used to go along too. Mark always wanted me with him. I was the only wife allowed out with them. I didn't stop them having a couple of drinks and dancing naked on the table – that was just part of it. A lot of the other wives didn't like their husbands drinking too much and taking off their clothes, but I let them crack on. I was the only wife in the "jolly boys club" – which was basically the rugby club – and I was the only girl in the club allowed to go on tour, because I didn't try to chaperone them or parent them. I acted like a child too.

The whistle blew for the end of the match and the Harlequins had triumphed. Mark jogged over to us and lifted Tori up and swung her round, before giving me a kiss on the cheek. "You won, Daddy, you won!" Tori was skipping along beside him and he grinned down at her. His face and arms were smeared with mud and there was a bloody-looking graze on his knee.

"Daddy needs a shower. We'll meet him in the bar," I said.

Mark reached up and rubbed his forehead.

"What was wrong with that bloke? He was bang out of order, punching you like that," I said.

Mark nodded. "I warned him – shame I couldn't get the ref to hear me… He went down quite hard."

A couple of other players came up and slapped him on the back and they all disappeared into the changing area. At home later, Mark told me how they had found all their bags had been rifled through in the changing rooms at half-time, and phones and things had been taken. The team they had been playing against had left a bad impression, but we didn't realize worse was to come.

* * *

"A mosquito net? Why would I have seen your mosquito net?"

I could hear a cupboard being pulled open and the rustle of bags being unzipped. Mark was packing for exercise. It was a regular occurrence, but somehow there was always a panic to find a piece of kit that wasn't where he left it... or not where he thought he'd left it.

"Dinner is nearly ready," I called out. "Tori, can you wash your hands please and set the table?"

It was a good job we had a roomy flat for our enlarged family, now there were four of us. I spooned a small helping of everything into a plastic bowl and mashed it up with a fork and some gravy. Alix was standing holding on to the settee when I walked in. "Ooh, standing up, Alix!" I said with a smile. Scooping her up in my arms, I slid her into the high chair and put the bowl just out of her reach on the table.

Mark wandered in, scratching his head. "It's not there. I'll have to go back into work and see if it's with the kit in the office."

I was spooning out portions of vegetables onto the plates. "I hope you won't be long. We've hardly seen you this weekend and then you'll be away for weeks."

Mark was playing aeroplanes with Alix's food and both girls were giggling uncontrollably.

"Where is Belize?" Tori asked, tipping her head on one side.

Mark paused with a forkful of meat on its way to his mouth. "It's between North and South America. I'll show you on a map after dinner."

Tori rested her chin on her hand. "Would I like it there?"

"It's mostly jungle, so there are lots of things that bite. That's why I've got to sleep under a net to keep them out."

She didn't want him to go. I could see that. She always asked where he was going and wanted to look it up on the map.

"We should get a world map, Mark, and put it up in the

kitchen – we can put in pins for where you've been and where we've been."

Mark nodded. "We can put in all the places we want to visit too – the capital cities."

I smiled cynically. "If you're ever home long enough, that would be good!"

* * *

I wasn't expecting many calls from Mark while he was away this time. I knew jungle training meant communication would be minimal. My coursebooks were stacked ominously at the end of the table and I promised myself one cup of coffee before I delved into reading for the next essay. Just as I heard the kettle humming loudly, the phone started to ring. I wondered for a moment if it might be Mark, but then I heard the voice of his rugby coach from the Harlequins. "Evening, Brenda." He didn't sound his usual breezy self. I explained that Mark was away on exercise and not due back for another eight weeks. He cleared his throat, which wasn't a good sign. "It's hit the fan," he said. "That player who hit Mark last week has now pressed charges and Mark may have to appear before the Rugby Football Union board."

My heart sank, and part of me felt angry too. *How could Mark be charged when the other guy started hitting him first?* The coach told me Mark would have to report to Hounslow police station on his return from Belize.

I couldn't contact Mark, and wasn't sure I would want to anyway, but the next evening he made a rare phone call. The signal was poor, but I was just able to explain about the charges and how serious it sounded.

"There's nothing I can do till I'm home, Brenda."

"I know. It's ridiculous, Mark. I can't believe it."

It was a brief phone call, but I lay in bed a few hours later unable to sleep. *What if this goes further? Will it go to court?* Having to appear at a police station sounded very serious. My stomach was churning and I couldn't get the fears of where it might lead out of my head. Mark wasn't a thug. He wasn't unjust either. He was straight as a die, but no one could push him around because he wouldn't take prisoners. He'd been a real street fighter in his younger days, but that was in the past. *Surely his exemplary record in the army would make them throw out any allegations of assault?*

But I was wrong.

When he returned from exercise, we discovered he was facing criminal charges for grievous bodily harm with intent. It was then the awful gravity of the situation began to sink in. We'd been warned that if he were to be found guilty, Mark could face dishonourable discharge from the army and the loss of his pension. The repercussions seemed to be snowballing out of control. I still couldn't believe the case would go ahead. We later discovered Mark should have put in a counterclaim, because he had been assaulted first. But he tried to fight his case, putting in mitigating evidence for what he'd done. He was just being honest.

Several weeks later, after Mark had appeared before the RFU and had been banned for twenty-eight matches, the coach phoned again for an update on the proceedings. We'd heard from our solicitor that the player who had made the complaint had claimed he was suffering from frequent headaches and was frightened to go out at night. The coach informed us he must have made a good recovery because he was playing professional rugby again. This made us both feel even worse. We knew it would be some months before the case came to trial, and the uncertainty hung over us both like a dark cloud. In the meantime, we were on the move again.

* * *

The noise around the pool was beginning to give me a headache. There were shouts and screams from the children standing at the sides, and the throbbing of the heaters and splashing of the water were pounding like a drumbeat in my head. I could see Alix was beginning to drop off and I stood up and rocked the buggy gently as her eyelids fluttered. Beyond the rail around the seating area Mark was crouched at the poolside in his running gear. He'd come straight from the gym and was waving his arm at Tori as she ploughed up the lane in what looked like a very competent crawl. *Better than I could do anyway!* He had a stopwatch in his hand and strode along to the end of the pool, crouching down again as she paused to look up at him. He'd told me she was a good swimmer and he wanted to encourage her. But it was an effort to come twice a week. He wasn't always free to do the ferrying and face the changing room.

I felt slightly wistful today about the pool. We now had a date for our next move. The regiment was heading to Northern Ireland for two years. Although I had loved living in London, part of me was happy to be going home. We'd be able to spend more time with my parents, who were becoming more and more frail, and Tori and Alix would also get to know their extended family in Northern Ireland. But I would miss the buzz of the city and all the treats we'd enjoyed as part of Mark's public duties, which had included tickets to Wimbledon. That wasn't going to happen in Ballykilner!

We hadn't talked to Tori much about the move yet. We'd dropped a hint about how it might be nice to live near the sea and nearer her Northern Irish grandparents and cousins. The trouble was, at nine years old she was very settled in her school. And I had my teaching assistant job there and it was a lovely place to work. She didn't need me around, because she had a good set of friends and seemed so happy. I was dreading the day she had to say goodbye.

After leaving Mark with Alix, I went to check on Tori in the changing room. I found her in the shower, where she was chatting happily to another girl, who was also at her school. They giggled as they slid around on the tiles at their feet. "Come on, Tori, hurry up and rinse your hair," I scolded.

Over in the spectator area Mark was pushing the buggy back and forth. He didn't know I was watching. He was looking down at Alix sleeping and I could see from his face he was enjoying the moment. Even in the midst of the clamour all around, he was admiring his beautiful sleeping baby.

"Where's my towel, Mummy?" screeched Tori. I bundled her up in the dry towel and we padded round to the changing rooms.

"Daddy said I did my best time today! Did you know?"

"I know. That's great, Tori – fantastic."

March 2002

I stood by the doorway to the classroom and watched Tori gather up papers and pictures and drop them into a bag. She looked downhearted, and I felt emotional myself. I'd said goodbye to the school staff a couple of weeks ago as I'd had to finish work a bit earlier. I was used to this moving around; it was a way of life. For the first time in our married life we had decided to pay for cleaners, so the clinical house cleaning wasn't really necessary, as Mark kept telling me, but I couldn't resist doing a certain amount anyway. At least this move we'd be able to use the oven until we left without worrying. Army "march-outs" were a serious business, and Mark and I were pretty good at them. We had a system. Mark did the cooker and I cleaned the windows, which included all the crevices and the sills. Everything had to be spotless, from plugholes to the tops of doors. But with two young children, one of whom was still a toddler, we'd decided having cleaners would save us some stress, because we had a long journey to make this time. We were driving back to Northern Ireland via Scotland and the Stranraer ferry, with an overnight stop in the Midlands.

"I'm so sorry to be losing Tori," said a piercing voice beside me. Tori's class teacher was very slender, with a bohemian dress sense. Today she was in a flowing floral skirt in purples and greens. She was standing next to me, holding Tori's hand. I smiled and said, "Yes, we're all sad to be leaving."

Tori looked up at me and I could see she was close to tears. A little huddle of her friends were gathered a few desks away. "They gave me some presents, Mummy," she said in a faltering voice. I took her hand and thanked her teacher and then had to pause while the posse of friends ran forward and hugged her in a mini rugby scrum.

As we walked toward the gate, she was silent. She glanced back at her friends who were waving. The tears started to roll as soon as she was in the car, and Mark turned to her before pulling out into the road. "Was it a good day, Tori?"

"I…. I… why do we have to move? I don't want to move to Ireland. Why can't we stay? I won't know anyone there."

Then she started to sob in earnest. I turned round and patted her leg and said, "It will be OK, sweetie, honestly." Alix stared at her from her baby seat, a little furrow appearing on her brow.

"Tori, stop crying, you're upsetting Alix."

"I… I… I can't."

When the car pulled up outside the flats, Mark had a stony expression on his face. He pulled open the passenger door and picked Tori up in his arms and carried her up to the flat. Once we'd put out the iced fingers I'd bought and turned on the TV, her sobbing subsided. He was filling the kettle at the sink, while I stood in the doorway. "I'm never doing that to her again, Brenda. We can't do this again."

I nodded. I didn't know what that would mean, but I understood. Changing schools every two years might be OK for some children, but not ours.

"'I don't have worries and I don't believe in crises.'
That was the Mark Hale approach.
He was better read, better informed, more articulate,
and more astute than all of us."

Major (now Lieutenant Colonel) Darren Denning

CHAPTER 11

July 2002: Northern Ireland

... a time to grieve

So much for the blue skies of summer, I thought as I gazed up at the gathering clouds outside. The pile of washing would have to go in the dryer again because I couldn't risk hanging it out while rain threatened.

"This is what it's like in Ireland," I muttered to myself, wishing we were back in London or the south of England, where the sun always seemed to appear on the weather maps. As I laid the breakfast things out on the table, my mood matched the weather. The previous evening we had talked again about the case, and began to map out the worst possible outcomes.

"What if they find you guilty, Mark?" I said in a hushed voice. Somehow, saying it made it too real. Both the children were in bed, but our voices remained hushed. We didn't want Tori to hear our discussions. We were sitting at the table with coursework books spread out around us. I watched him press his fingers down the spine of the book, flattening out the pages.

"If it all goes wrong, Brenda, we have the house in Bangor.

You and the girls will be OK. We'll stop renting it out and you'll be able to move in there if you have to leave the quarter." He took a deep breath and looked across at me. Neither of us wanted to contemplate the consequences. He placed his hand on mine and squeezed it. "We've been broke before; we would just have to do it again."

I nodded. "I know. I know that, Mark."

"We'll have each other. As long as we're all together – you, me, and the girls – that's what really matters, isn't it?"

The case was already costing us hundreds of pounds, as Mark had to travel back to London for various court appearances, and the date of the hearing kept being changed. We were so grateful for the support of a few close friends who knew what was happening. The Padre and Mark's former Commanding Officer, Lt Col Richard Toomey, had given unstinting support, as had Roger Cleave, Mark's boss. We couldn't talk about what was happening to anyone except our closest friends. It felt like a dark secret burden that we carried, and at times I thought it was going to crush me completely. We didn't want the charges to affect Mark's next confidential report and his future career, so the whole thing was being kept very much under wraps.

The case wasn't my only worry. I was anxious about my mummy. She'd been diagnosed with heart disease some time earlier, but recently she'd become increasingly breathless. She struggled to look after the children and I always had to stay when we visited, although she wanted so much to spend time with them. I'd said I would take them over to see her today, and my sister had called earlier to say I should come to the hospital.

Half an hour later Tori was lounging on the settee with Alix cuddled against her. "Come on, girls," I said. "You need to get dressed and get your teeth done; we're going out soon to see Grandma." I had picked up a clean pair of leggings and a T-shirt and started helping Alix into them when my mobile phone started vibrating. I looked down and saw it was Mark and it showed two other missed calls from him. Once I'd got Alix's clothes on, I pressed his number.

I knew he was busy down on the Garvaghy Road. It was the time of the July parades and it was all kicking off this month.

"Mark, what d'you want?" I said.

"You need to get to Bangor quick."

"I know. Alison's phoned me. I'm on my way."

"Brenda, it's your mum."

"I know, I know. I'll be down in a bit. I'm getting the girls ready."

"No, you need to be in Bangor now, Brenda... your mummy's died."

I felt myself go numb as his words sank in. My sister hadn't wanted to tell me over the phone, so she'd called Mark instead. They thought he could handle me better! As I ended the call, I went into automatic pilot. I barely felt the spots of rain as I bundled the girls into the car and strapped Alix into her seat. As I drove to the hospital, I wondered how on earth to break the news to Tori as she sat in the back of the car totally unaware.

I could hardly trust myself to speak, so I started to talk about something else until I eventually said, "Grandma is really, really ill. We don't know, she may be with Jesus by the time we get to see her."

Tori nodded and her eyes widened. She didn't say anything but she reached out her hand and held Alix's. I felt a lump forming in my throat; the little gesture meant so much.

After I'd said my farewells to my mummy and spent some time with my daddy and my sisters and brother, we headed out to the car. The rain had stopped, and as I swung the car around the lane and toward the barracks, a huge rainbow appeared in front of us, shimmering across the partly clearing skies.

"Oh, look, that's my grandma smiling at me from heaven," said Tori.

Tears sprang to my eyes. "Yes, that's beautiful, isn't it? Grandma is with Jesus now." But even as I said the words, I felt the loss and the loneliness seep through me. She'd gone, and I wouldn't be able to phone her up and ask her advice or hear her soothing voice. I felt silent tears sliding down my face and I didn't even bother to wipe them away.

* * *

The iron spluttered and hissed as the steam puffed out onto the crisp cotton of the white shirt. I pressed it hard into the corners of the cuffs, trying to make a perfect job. When it was finished, I reached for a hanger and began to fasten the buttons one by one.

"Which tie will you wear?"

He looked up from where he was sitting and his eyes seemed blank, as if he didn't understand what I was saying.

"Tie... you know, you'll have to wear one in court?"

"I... probably just a plain one."

"Not the regimental tie?"

He hesitated. "I'm not sure. I'll take both."

I needed to be busy because I was finding it hard to face the next few days. Mark would be flying back to London tomorrow for the hearing the following day. It felt as if our lives were hanging in the balance, waiting to be counted. We didn't even know if he would be coming back. Being sent to prison was a real possibility. I was scared. Scared about what the next few days might bring.

When he left the house the next day and I heard the door close, I suddenly felt so alone. Losing my mum a few months earlier had been an awful blow, and we were all concerned about my daddy. We were fairly sure he was showing signs of Alzheimer's disease. Half the time he didn't seem to know what was going on, which was so unlike him. He'd had a sharp mind, and it was through him I'd thrashed out my political views. We had discussed current affairs at length. Although we saw things differently, I had huge respect for his opinions.

I felt as if I was too young to lose my parents. I wasn't mature enough to cope with life without them at the end of the phone. Now I was frightened that I could be losing Mark too. It was a terrible prospect. It was unbearable for him to consider that he might lose the job he loved and had worked so tirelessly to succeed in. I prayed silently that God would help us and that this wouldn't be the end for Mark in the army.

As we were lying in bed the previous night, Mark had turned toward me, and his face had looked pained. "I'm not a criminal."

"Of course you're not," I snapped. "That guy deserved a beating. I would…"

"Ssh…" he said, putting his fingers against my lips, but he was smiling too. "They'd better not let you get your hands on him. He'll need protection!"

He always teased me that I'd only married him so that I had someone to boss around, but he was wrong. He was the strong one, the one I leaned on, and the one I looked to. I couldn't bear the thought of him not coming back to us.

* * *

I lined up the fish fingers on the foil and slid the tray under the grill. *Surely it must be over*, I thought. I wanted the phone to ring, but I was terrified at the same time. I was trying to keep things as normal as possible for the children. Tori was sitting with a friend on the lounge carpet playing Guess Who with the pop-up characters, while they tried to distract Alix with a tower of Duplo to stop her ruining their game.

"It will be dinner soon, girls."

They glanced up and nodded. Alix stood up and started tottering toward the Christmas tree where a bright gold bauble was hanging just out of reach. I dodged my way around the obstacles on the floor and scooped her up just before she reached the branches. "Come on, Alix, let's get you in your chair," I said.

Thank goodness the children are here to keep me busy. Just after I'd wriggled Alix into her high chair and given her a breadstick to chew on, the phone started to ring. My insides were somersaulting as I put the receiver to my ear.

"Brenda."

"Mark, are you OK?"

"I'm coming home. We'll talk about it when I get home."

I sighed. "Thank God, Mark. Thank God for that."

He didn't fill me in on all the details until later, but the big thing was he was coming home, and for Christmas. As I sank onto the chair in front of Alix I started to sob, big tears of relief flooding down my face. It had been more than a year since the charge had been brought, and finally it seemed it was over. The fact that he was coming home meant that, no matter what the court had handed out in judgment, we would deal with it.

The final ruling was unjust. The prosecutors had dropped the "intent" and Mark was found guilty of GBH. He was given a suspended sentence and ordered to do two hundred hours of community service, as well as to pay a fine. This result was largely due to of the testimonials from senior army officers. His previous Commanding Officer, our very good friend Richard Toomey, and the Padre were both character witnesses in court. The Padre was a rugby referee and spoke glowingly about Mark. They both talked about his exemplary record, his morals, and his leadership, as well as the way he inspired others and was a role model to younger soldiers. The solicitor said their powerful testimonies had saved him from a harsher sentence.

The community service was served working behind the bar in the regimental sports club, where he already volunteered. It was mainly served during the Rugby World Cup, which England went on to win. He would open up the bar each day and ended up being able to watch every match. It felt as if God had a strange way of answering our prayers.

*"He had that magic touch of adding calm
and a sense of perspective
whilst all around would be losing their head."*

Major Mark Owen

Chapter 12

2004: Northern Ireland

... a time to dream

The doors of the removal van slammed shut and there was a rumble as the lorry pulled away. I had a nostalgic pang as I looked around the empty kitchen. Unlike most quarter kitchens with wonky cupboards and drawers in cheap Formica, this house had a brand new kitchen which I'd enjoyed for the past two years. It was in fact the best army quarter we'd ever had – a nice red-brick detached house which sat beside the church. But the speckled lino in the kitchen was still a nightmare to clean, and the only way to remove marks was down on your hands and knees with a scourer and a cloth. The ancient white electric cooker was the hallmark of all military homes. It was winking at me today, its silver rings sparkling in the sunlight streaming in through crystal clear windows. *Why is it our houses only look fantastic when we are leaving?*

It was set to be our last "march-out" for some time because we were moving to our own house at last. Three pairs of shoes were lined up by the front door and I could hear Mark trailing round upstairs with the girls as they went from room to room. I stood at the bottom of the stairs and watched them trudge down, each of the girls holding one of his hands. They collapsed in a heap a few steps from the bottom and grinned at me.

"We've been checking they haven't left any toys or valuables behind," he explained.

I raised my eyebrows. "I still have some cleaning to do from where all the furniture's been. Why don't you take them round to the park for half an hour and I can…"

"I thought we were going to the new house?" interrupted Tori. "Aren't we going there now, Daddy?" She looked up at him with pleading eyes. Mark ruffled her hair and Alix crawled onto his lap and wrapped her arms around his neck. When he stood up, she clung to him like a monkey, encircling his waist with her legs.

"Come on, Tori – unless you want to stay and help clean?"

She shook her head and gave the dormant hoover a wide berth, as if it were likely to pounce. She was eleven going on sixteen and that autumn would be starting secondary school. She had a place at Victoria College, an all-girls' school in Belfast, which also took boarders.

We had discussed the future and our daughters' education at length after the move from Twickenham. Mark had done some research into girls and education through some of his psychology studies and he'd discovered girls generally learn better in a single-sex school. We had also decided we would stay in our own house as long as possible, postings permitting. The hope was that Tori would be well settled in the new school before a posting took us away. By that time she would be used to boarding during the week so the transition to full-time boarding wouldn't be so hard, as she would have established friendships and be that bit older. Our plan was to rent out the new house if necessary during any long postings to the UK or further afield. Mark and I couldn't face living apart; there was enough separation in the army as it was.

As I trundled round the house with the hoover and cleaning cloths – one wet and one dry to prevent smears – I did feel a little sad. We had enjoyed two years here on the "patch", where the children were safe to play in the road and run in and out of one another's homes. There had been good mutual support among the wives and there was always someone to ask for help if you needed it. Abercorn Barracks was set in a perfect location right next to the sea, and we'd spent many happy afternoons and days playing on the beach, watching Mark with his kite buggy racing across the golden sand, and often sheltering from the blustery westerlies behind a windbreak.

I pulled open the fitted wardrobes and pushed the hoover nozzle into the corners, then reached up to the high cupboards. The suction made a strange noise as a large piece of paper stuck against the end of the pipe. I pulled it off to check it was nothing important. It was a photocopied leaflet on back exercises from Hedley Court. I flattened it out and laid it on the windowsill. Mark was doing better now, but his back injury had been terrible at the time. He never complained about pain – that wasn't his way. I'd watched him crawl out of bed in the mornings after his operation. They had shaved some discs in his back to stop the pain. Before the operation he couldn't even drive because he couldn't feel his feet.

Flipping rugby! The game's had a lot to answer for over the past few years. It was playing rugby that had caused the injury, and Mark had just carried on, trying to ignore it. He'd been on a lot of painkillers and the doctors couldn't believe he was still playing rugby. He was sent to Hedley Court to have some special back rehab. They had said it was only because he had such a strong core that he was able to make such a good recovery. But the injury had changed his fitness regime. Now he focused more on exercises that didn't put so much pressure on his spine, like cycling and the rower, rather than running. He was still fanatical about fitness, and his collection of road bikes was growing. Somehow we would need to make space for his kit in the new house.

We'd decided it was the right time to buy our own house, and then soon after, we heard that Mark was to be Garrison Sergeant Major (GSM) at the HQ for Northern Ireland in Lisburn. That meant two more years in Northern Ireland, which was just what we needed – a bit of stability after all the stress of the past couple of years. Dromara was in the right place for us both to get into work easily, as I now had a job as a residential social worker in Downpatrick.

Mark had been pleased about being made GSM, but I knew what he really wanted was to be Regimental Sergeant Major for the regiment. That was the top prize for any soldier who had worked their way up from a Private. Mark had been very pragmatic. He'd said it was a good job and explained his responsibilities, which encompassed the whole of the Garrison, based at the army's HQ. There was a possibility he could be offered a commission as an officer, and everyone was saying he was bound to "pick up" as they called it, but it hadn't happened so far. If that didn't pan out, we had other plans. Mark never took anything for granted, which is why he was still studying hard. Once he'd completed his psychology degree, he was planning to start a Master's degree. He'd have plenty to offer potential employers when he left the army, and with our own home, we'd have a secure base, whatever happened.

A few hours later we were in. After the removal men had finished swigging their tea and shut the door behind them, I collapsed on the bottom step of the newly carpeted stairs and surveyed the sea of boxes and furniture. I felt Mark sink down behind me, and seconds later Tori threw herself against my legs, followed by Alix. I leaned back against Mark's legs and laughed. "Our own house at last!"

Both girls nestled in beside us so that Mark could envelop us all in a kind of rugby hug. "What d'you think, girls? Do you like the new house?"

"I love my bedroom," said Tori.

Alix just smiled contentedly.

"And the garden," Tori added. "I like the garden – it's posh."

"I like the kitchen best," I said. "No lino or grotty cupboards, and a proper cooker!"

"When is tea?" said Alix.

We all laughed. Given she was the smallest member of the family, her appetite was incredible.

"How about fish and chips?" Mark suggested.

"Yeee!" Both the girls jumped up and did a little jig in the hallway. Mark slid his arms around me and whispered, "Is that OK with you, Mrs Hale?"

It would be a few days before we were actually living in the house. My old college friend Alyson, who lived opposite, had offered to put us all up until we'd finished the decorating. All the furniture and boxes were moved into the middle of the rooms and Mark worked until dark each day painting, starting with the girls' bedrooms. Each of them had chosen the colour they wanted. It was such a change to have something other than magnolia, the regulation shade for all army quarters. Alix had specifically requested "lellow", as she said it, and the room now had a real sunshine feel.

Both the girls were round at Alyson's, which gave me a chance to start to unpack boxes in the rooms that were ready. It was strange to be living outside the wire in Northern Ireland. It went against the grain. Living within the barracks was more secure, but

I took some comfort from the fact that there was a police station at the end of the road. Still, we were careful not to publicize that Mark was in the army.

Decorating was taking its toll on Mark's back injury. The next evening I found him lying on the floor in the bedroom at Alyson's house, and I could tell from his eyes he was in pain. I knelt down beside him. He was in an old khaki T-shirt that was now splattered with white paint, and even his hair was speckled with white from the spray off the roller.

"You're a mess, honey."

"I know. You're going to have to help me, Bren... I can't move." He smiled through gritted teeth.

"Daddy! Daddy!" came a high-pitched voice from the landing, and Alix trotted in excitedly. She ran toward him and jumped straight onto his chest, leaping around, while Mark winced.

"Alix! Daddy's back's hurting!" I said, as I scooped her off. She flopped down beside him and watched as I hauled him to his feet and he swigged back a couple more painkillers before gingerly walking toward the shower. It was a miracle he managed to finish the decorating, but he was a fighter, and a bit of back pain wasn't going to stop him completing his mission.

July 2005

Boxes were lined up on the kitchen table and I was carefully packing cereal boxes and biscuits, trying to use as little space as possible. I stood back and wondered how we were going to fit it all in the car. Alix appeared in the doorway, dragging a tiny wetsuit behind her. "I'm packing," she said.

"Good, that's great. Well done. Take that to Daddy out by the car."

"I've got to find my bucket first. He said we need it." Then she reached up and pulled open the back door.

I glanced at my watch. *Why does time speed up when you're packing to leave?* It was 11 a.m. already and I needed to give everyone lunch before we left.

"*Bonjour, Madame,*" said a disembodied voice from behind the door.

"*Bonjour,* Tori!" I replied. "Have you finished packing your bag?"

A head popped round the door, then an arm and a leg. "Alix has packed all her teddies in the suitcase and I can't fit any clothes in!"

I sighed. Something told me we were going to be late for the ferry.

We were off to France for a three-week holiday at a campsite in the Vendée. Everyone was excited. I carried a packed box out to the drive where Mark was loading things into the new roof box.

"Here's one box of food," I said, dumping it on the ground beside the car. "It's great we've got a top box for all the suitcases and things. We should have plenty of room inside this time."

Mark pulled the lid down and glanced at the box. "Suitcases?"

"Yes, suitcases for our clothes, Mark. We have to have clothes – we're away for three weeks."

He peered into the car. "We'll put them on the back seat. The top box has all the kite buggy stuff in it; I can't fit anything else in."

I didn't say anything. I just turned and went back to the kitchen. His kit always came first. He'd just have to find a way to fit in what we needed somehow.

In the end we made the journey crushed in with suitcases around our legs. At least there was time to stretch on the ferries to Liverpool and Cherbourg, and we enjoyed a few days with Dianne and Roger in Poole en route.

* * *

The crunch of wheels on gravel signalled that Mark was back from his early morning cycle. I stretched and reached for my towel and the beach bag. Tori was playing with Alix on the rug outside. It was a game of snap that sounded loud and full of giggles.

"How are my girls?" Mark appeared round the side of the tent, his face gleaming with sweat, sunglasses pushed to the top of his head.

"Daddy! Daddy's back!" two high-pitched voices shouted, and Alix ran toward him and threw herself around his legs. Tori smiled across at him. "You can play now, Daddy. I'm just about to deal."

A partly demolished French stick lay on the little camping table. Mark broke off a chunk and started biting into it.

"We had our breakfast ages ago," said Alix. "Can I have some too?"

I walked toward them and patted Alix's head. "There's more bread in the box. I'm sure Daddy will help you find some food." Turning to Mark I said, "There are eggs and bacon if you want them in the fridge. See you all in a bit."

"Have a nice swim," he said.

Ploughing up and down the pool was very therapeutic on holiday. It gave me some space and time to myself. That was usually how we managed the days. Mark got his fitness sessions in early and then came back and gave me a break. After lunch we'd head out all together, usually to the beach or to explore somewhere. We were really enjoying France this time. The weather had been good. The beaches weren't too packed and the countryside was lush. On the way there, we'd visited the house of former French President Georges Clemenceau, with its fascinating treasures and history, and also Monet's house and gardens where we'd seen the famous lily pond and bridge. The paths in the garden ran between flowerbeds overflowing with colour, and all around were idyllic views of bright petals drooping over winding paths and bees humming through the blooms. We both felt there was something very special about France.

"I think we should buy a house here after I leave the army," Mark had announced a couple of days earlier, as we sat at a café in a quaint village square.

"We'd all have to learn French."

The girls were stroking a scraggy-looking donkey that had appeared a few minutes earlier, pulling a little cart. An old man in blue overalls with a bright neckerchief tied at his throat had secured its reins to a post opposite the café and he was unloading boxes of vegetables from the back of the wagon.

"I suppose we should work out where about in France we'd want to be." I swished the remains of my coffee around the little white cup. Mark was watching the girls with the donkey.

"The quality of life would be good here. It would be good for the girls too… they could learn another language."

As I came to the end of the pool again, I kicked off hard with my feet and felt myself glide through the water. *I wonder if we could make the move here.* It seemed a far-off dream, but Mark actually only had a few years left, unless he was commissioned, and that was never certain. We'd both finished our degrees now and Mark hoped to begin a Master's next. There were plenty of jobs he could do after the army. He was still relatively young. I felt quite excited at the prospect. *Who knows what the future holds?*

* * *

Waves were rushing in across the wide stretch of sand and I knew they would have to abandon the kite buggy soon, as there would be no beach left to race along. I stretched out my legs and enjoyed the feeling of heat on my skin, which was gradually turning a slightly darker shade of pale. My skin was not the tanning kind, unlike Mark's, which would begin to turn golden with the slightest sniff of sunshine. He always teased me about my pale legs, and today had been no exception. I'd finally decided to go for a swim, and as we all splashed in the shallows, Mark had turned to me and said, "Be careful, Brenda, it's the whale mating season!"

I'd kicked the water up at him and told him to shut up. The girls had been screaming and splashing him too, and we'd all headed into the waves.

The waves had been quite small that afternoon, but were getting larger now that the tide was rushing in. The book I was reading had got a bit slow. I pressed the corner down at the top of the page and slid it into the beach bag. A little girl dressed in a red and white spotty costume was tottering past, holding a plastic spade. She was staring at her feet, and every few metres she squatted down to pick up a shell and gaze at it. I wondered where her parents were – she couldn't have been much more than three or four, perhaps a little younger than Alix.

Further across the beach, shouts and laughter from the trio with the kite buggy were floating across with each little gust of wind. Mark had Alix in his arms and was steering the buggy right and left as it veered from side to side with each fresh gust of wind. Tori was running behind them, shouting, "My turn! My turn!" They never tired of playing with their dad, and he was so patient at teaching them anything, from building sandcastles to flying kites. I reached for my top, slid my arms inside, and zipped it up. The wind was whipping up spray from the incoming waves, showering water like a sprinkler onto the damp sand below.

The little girl had stopped now and was staring across at me. *Is she searching for her mummy?* She wasn't crying. Someone was calling out from further along the beach. I could see a figure walking rapidly in my direction, their head turning from side to side. It was a woman, and now she was almost running. As she came fully into view, I could see she was dressed in a long, striped T-shirt. She paused and looked across at the lone child who had turned in her direction. Then the woman started running toward her, and seconds later she knelt down and wrapped her arms around the lost child. I smiled and jumped to my feet. It was time to herd my tribe back. I was glad she had found her daughter, and it had made me want to be with mine. I wanted to wrap my arms around them too and enjoy that feeling of knowing we were all together, all safe.

* * *

The smell of freshly cooked pancakes was intoxicating. As we trailed up the path from the beach each day, laden with bags of towels and damp clothes, we rarely made it past the van selling chocolate crêpes. Without even checking with us, the girls scrambled onto white plastic chairs and propped their elbows on the table, looking expectantly at Mark and me.

"What kind of crêpes would you like, girls?"

We knew the answer before it came back, like an echo in unison: "Chocolate, chocolate..." they chanted.

As we sat around the table a few minutes later, with chocolate-smeared faces and empty plates, Mark picked up the menu and quizzed Tori with French words. "Not bad, Tori," he said, satisfied that she seemed to have learned some new words over the past few days. "Tonight we'll let you order your meal in French!"

She giggled and said, *"Merci, Monsieur!"* Seconds later Alix chimed in with the echo, *"Merci... Merci..."* We all collapsed in laughter and Alix continued to chant her new word, to the amusement of new arrivals at the beach café.

"Mark Hale did fill a room and proved that you don't have to be noisy to do so. He cared for his people, and such was the respect in which he was held that formality was never needed in his command."

Major (now Lieutenant Colonel) Darren Denning

CHAPTER 13

2006: Dromara, Northern Ireland

... a time to treasure

"Brenda..."

"Yes, what's the problem?"

"I've got a puncture... Can you come and get me?"

I sighed, but said, "Of course," jotting down where he was. It was about half an hour's drive away and luckily he'd given me the route he was taking before he left. It was a Saturday morning and I'd been giving the house a blitz while Tori was out at a friend's house and Alyson was minding Alix. Having called in and picked up Alix, I lifted the bike rack into the car and we were soon sweeping round the bends into the countryside. I could see Alix's eyes already beginning to close. *She'll be asleep in a second.*

I wasn't quite sure how far Mark had cycled today, but I knew it was often about seventy or eighty miles. He'd think nothing of it. He loved being on the bike and he'd come back exhausted but buzzing. I was only just getting used to having him around for a few weeks since he'd returned from Iraq, and he'd soon be off again for his Late Entry Officers Course (LEOC) at the Royal

Military Academy, Sandhurst, back in the UK. We were pleased he'd been picked up for a commission, but the news came tinged with sadness because he'd just started his time as Regimental Sergeant Major (RSM).

* * *

I pictured his face on the day he'd heard he had got RSM. He was like the cat that got the cream or a child at Christmas – completely hyper. He appeared round the back door at the end of the afternoon. I had heard his bike crunching on the gravel, so I knew he was home. He had this big goofy smile and his eyes were gleaming. He picked me up and swung me round, and when he put me down, he kissed me.

"I'm going back as RSM! My name is going to be on that board, Brenda… it's going to be up there in the Mess. Regimental Sergeant Major Mark Hale – 1st Battalion the Devonshire and Dorset Regiment. You can't get better than that!"

I'd already put a bottle of champagne in the fridge and I was about to slide a big fillet of beef into the oven. We celebrated in style. I knew this was what Mark had always wanted. This had been his goal and at last he'd achieved it. By the end of the evening we were both a bit wobbly as we swayed up the stairs to the bedroom.

The downside was that he would have to go to Catterick, where the regiment was based under its new name – the Devonshire and Dorset Light Infantry (D&D LI). As they were due to deploy to Iraq in the spring, there was no point in all of us moving. We coped with the separation and he flew home every other weekend, and we made the trip there as often as we could.

He'd only been RSM for six weeks when he received the news that he'd been picked up for a commission as an officer. It was good news and gave us several more years' stability in a job he loved, but for Mark it was also a blow. He'd been looking forward to deploying on operations as RSM – a job that would normally last about two years. Now he would be going as Captain Hale, the Regimental Careers Management Officer (RCMO). Although he was disappointed, he was still able to joke about it.

"The thing is, Brenda, I could do in six weeks what it takes others two years to do!" It was the usual positive spin. He was also aware it would be the D&Ds' last operational tour before they were amalgamated into the big regiment – The Rifles – so the promotion to officer was a very bittersweet pill.

* * *

When I reached the pull-in, with some last-minute direction over the phone, Mark was leaning against his bike, holding his helmet in his hands. Muscles were etched on every limb, the Lycra suit moulding itself around his body like a second skin. After fitting his bike onto the rack, he slid into the passenger seat and swigged from his water bottle. "That was going well; shame about the tyre."

I looked down at his knee, which was sporting a dark gash of what looked like dried blood and grit. "Did you fall?"

"Only for you..." he grinned.

* * *

I heard bits and pieces about the tour when he came back from Iraq. I gathered it had been slightly different in his new role, although I didn't think Mark had changed. He was still the same tough soldier with a sharp sense of humour. One of his friends told me about his plan to make his hair self-cleaning during the tour – perhaps thinking of saving water in the desert. He'd read something about how it wasn't necessary to wash it because after a few weeks it would "clean itself". Without me around to march him into the shower, I suppose it was his only chance to put the theory to the test. According to the lads it was very smelly for a few weeks and then it apparently worked. That didn't stop me making him get straight in the shower when he got home, to use shampoo.

Despite the demands of the tour, Mark had managed to complete the final assignment of his Master's degree during the deployment. He'd told me about a missile coming in while he was sitting the final exam, which made the achievement even more amazing. Now he was going back to the classroom for his officer's course. I had no fears that he would struggle, especially as he was applying to start a PhD looking at post-traumatic stress disorder.

One thing that had happened since Iraq was that Mark seemed to have a slightly different perspective on time and family. We'd been able to use Instant Messenger while he was away. It meant there was immediacy to our communication that we hadn't had before. One afternoon we were chatting and the line went dead. I thought he'd just hung up. But when he came back online, he told me he had booked the flights to Venice for my birthday in January. It was only later that he told me there had been a direct hit and he had decided to book Venice because he thought, *I might not be alive to take her another time.* They'd all had to make wills before they left on the tour, which was a sobering task and one Mark hadn't taken lightly. I had tried not to dwell on the dangers, but every day he had been in my thoughts and prayers.

Mark had a fair bit of leave to fit in when he got back, so we decided to splash out and go on our first family skiing holiday in December. There was a lot to look forward to and I was hoping his four weeks on the course at Sandhurst would fly by. He obviously wasn't finding the work very taxing and phoned quite often to tell me the latest classroom stories. A day or two after he'd left, I was lying on the settee in my pyjamas. It had been a freezing November day and I'd had to scrape the ice off the car windscreen in the morning. I pulled my hoody sweat top around me more tightly and wished Mark was home to snuggle up to in bed later. Sipping a soothing hot chocolate, I comforted myself with the thought that he would be coming back at the weekend. The phone started ringing and I reached across, hoping it would be him.

"Hello, sweetheart," I trilled. "How's it going?"

We chatted about the girls and my work for a few minutes, and then he told me about a few of the others on the course. "We had our induction today. They asked what level of qualification we'd all achieved. And people were asked to put their hands up if they had O Levels and then A Levels," he said.

"So did you put your hand up?"

"No. They stopped at A Levels and I don't have any. I guess they think LE officers wouldn't have degrees!"

I knew he was playing them, because he didn't like the assumption that LE officers weren't very intelligent. But I felt a bit frustrated because I wanted them to know how clever he was.

When he came home at the weekend I heard more about the course. In between coursework, he said, he'd been called in for a meeting to discuss his assignments after handing in his third essay. We'd just finished breakfast and I poured us both a second cup of coffee, raising my eyebrows. "That sounds ominous…"

He gave a half-smile as he explained, "They said they couldn't find anything wrong with my essays; they didn't need to red pen them. Then one of them said, 'We don't understand as we think you may be getting extra help or outside help because you've already told us you haven't got any A Levels.' I said, 'No, I haven't.'"

I giggled as he continued. "They told me they had no other choice but to investigate, and I said, 'OK then.' They both seemed a bit taken aback and then one of them asked, 'Don't you have any formal qualifications, like NVQs or anything?'"

"Oh, Mark, you had to put them out of their misery?" I interrupted.

"I said, 'Well, I've just finished my Master's out in Iraq.' The guy's face dropped and he said, 'Master's degree?' I said, 'Yes, Master's degree. I'm in the process of applying for a PhD.' The guy said, 'We had no idea.' And I said, 'You didn't ask.'"

We were both laughing now. "You couldn't resist that, could you?"

He grinned. "They ended up telling me I was better qualified than most of them!"

It was no surprise that Mark achieved the top grade on the course, and afterwards the tutors asked his permission to use his essays as model examples for future students.

* * *

I stood mesmerized by the colours and the fine detail of the picture. "Amazing," I whispered. "It's so fantastic to see them here in Venice."

I turned to look up at Mark, who was also scanning the painting on the wall. It was Canaletto's Grand Canal looking north east from the Palazzo Balbi to the Rialto Bridge. The light pushing through between the scuds of grey and white clouds across a deep blue sky was breathtaking, and the artist had lit up a few of the buildings on the left of the water, their detailed architecture picked out in the sunlight.

"Daddy was right," I commented. "He pointed out the clarity of his work when he took me to the National Gallery years ago."

"He was talented," murmured Mark. He squeezed my hand and we stepped back from the painting. Canaletto had become my favourite artist and so this holiday was particularly special, and

Mark knew that. He wasn't hurrying me; he was being so patient. I was feeling totally indulged by him on this trip. Although it was January we enjoyed the winter sunshine as we walked hand in hand beside the canals and sat at cafés in the ancient squares and narrow streets. We walked miles, hunting out as many basilicas as we could find. I knew this wasn't quite Mark's thing, but he was letting me do what I loved, and I was soaking up the rich culture and history with every step.

As we leaned over yet another curved bridge and watched a sailor-suited gondolier paddling a Japanese couple along the canal, I looked at him sideways. "If we'd come a few months earlier, you could have offered to be Daniel Craig's body double."

He raised his sunglasses provocatively. "I have better hair than Daniel Craig."

"That's true, you do..." As another gondolier passed below us and leaned forward, sending the boat swishing through the water, I said, "D'you think it's hard to keep your balance doing the punting? It looks easy but I bet it isn't..."

Mark turned to look at me, a slow smile spreading across his face.

I continued, "No, I don't think it's a future job for you. We had enough trouble with skiing!"

He slid his arm around me and pushed me against the stones of the low wall. "What are you saying about my skiing, Brenda?"

I was convulsed with laughter and he was trying not to laugh too. Our first family skiing holiday a few weeks earlier had been amazing, but I'd spent most of my time doubled up with laughter watching Mark's attempts to learn. Balance and coordination were not his strong points. Learning to march and drill had been a huge challenge, and I knew he could only really dance after a bit to drink and if he was holding both my hands. He had thrown himself into learning to ski, and while Tori and I had picked it up quite quickly, he had been falling over every few minutes, knocking down instructors, ploughing into chairlifts, and frequently getting tangled up and ending up on the ground when he tried to show his lift pass at the turnstiles. He was a big, strong guy, but he wasn't ever going to master skiing gracefully down a slope. It was all about speed and then trying to stop before he did too much damage at the bottom. I really believe he spent more time lying in the snow than he did skiing over it.

"Whatever you say, Mark, it's the one thing I'm better than you at."

"OK," he said, "but you're smaller so that makes it easier…"

"Excuses, excuses…" I muttered as we strode toward the square. He gripped my hand again and my heart skipped a beat as I looked up at him. We'd been married nineteen years and it felt like no time at all. It was as if we were on our honeymoon and I thought, *I love you now even more than I did that day in the disco when we first kissed.*

September 2007

A clatter of wood on concrete echoed up from the boathouse. I turned to check on Alix, who was wobbling slightly on her bike, the stabilizers nudging over the uneven track at the edge of the building. As I rounded the corner, I slid off the saddle and watched her squeezing the brakes in concentration as she came to a halt next to me. We were just a few metres from the edge of the river. Down on our left, a number of Lycra-clad men were manoeuvring a huge rowing boat down the steps toward the water. As they reached the water's edge, they lowered it slowly into the dark stream as if it were a delicate piece of china. They were incredibly precious about the boats – I suppose they were pretty expensive and easily damaged. Mark was crouching beside the boat and was adjusting a seat in the centre, while another of the team steadied it, gripping the long metal bars that held the oars.

Tori hadn't yet appeared and I guessed she was still in the changing room, chatting to her friends. "Come on, Alix," I said. "We'll carry on down the river and I expect they'll soon be coming past."

She didn't move. Her head was tilted to the side and she was watching her dad as he stood up and stretched. I looked back across at Mark, who was showing off his rippling six-pack in the skintight top, his powerful thighs bulging through the rowing shorts. He grinned at us. "Enjoy your ride," he called across and winked at Alix.

We both pedalled off down the path beside the river. There was a favourite café not far along and we usually took a break there, especially if it was a chilly day, when we'd order hot chocolate. Today the weather was clear, and the afternoon had a hint of an Indian summer. The grasses alongside the bank had grown taller in the last couple of weeks, from the combination of showers and hot sun. There were waving reeds, and a waist-high sea of cow parsley was threatening to block our view of the River Lagan, which was sliding past like an enormous treacle snake.

We'd been coming down to the Belfast Boat Club for the past few months, ever since Tori had given up swimming. She'd announced she didn't want to do it any more, but Mark was keen for her to have a sport. I think he was disappointed she'd given up after years of training several times a week. He'd heard they wanted to train more young rowers for the Olympics and he thought Tori might enjoy it, so he'd volunteered to take her along for a trial. We'd all arrived to see what it was like, and while they were helping Tori into a wobbly boat for the first time with another young girl, one of the rowers had eyed up Mark, who was standing watching on the steps with his arms folded. He was in his dark jeans and pink shirt, but you could still tell he was built for sport.

"What about you? Do you fancy a go?" A wiry man in tight Lycra shorts and a bright top was addressing Mark.

He shrugged and then said, "I guess so, if you think I'll fit in the seats!"

They all chuckled, and about ten minutes later he was sliding into another boat.

Alix was hopping about on the edge of the steps. "Can I come too? Can I? Please, Daddy?"

He looked across at the other rower squatting down at the side, holding the boat steady. "Come on then, Alix; you can be cox," he said. Leaning over, he held out his arm and lifted her into the little seat at the front of the boat, as if she weighed no more than a feather. I remembered seeing the look of glee on her face; her smile was stretching from ear to ear.

"Just don't fall in, either of you," I said, waving them off.

And that was how it started. It didn't take long for them to see that Mark was a natural rower. He and Tori soon became active members and our weekends began to be scheduled around rowing. We'd go to church in the morning, have Sunday lunch, then Mark would take Tori rowing and then take her back to boarding school while Alix and I went home. But about three weeks later, when he came back after dropping Tori at school, a frown was creasing his forehead.

"I've made some tea – it's in the pot," I said.

He poured himself a mug and then began sipping it, still standing by the table. "It's not working. I don't like it."

I said, "What's not working? You don't want to row?"

He shook his head and moved across to sit in the chair opposite. Alix was curled up in another chair, her nose buried in a book.

"I can't row while you two are sitting in the house. We need to be together."

I shrugged. "I don't see..."

He straightened up suddenly, almost as if an idea had sprung him upright. "Next week we'll take the bikes and you and Alix can ride along the towpath."

"So we're on the sidelines again watching you having fun rowing?"

He gave me that everlasting grin. It was what my life was like. I often told Mark, "I spend my time watching you have fun!" Whether it was on the rugby pitch or now on the river, Mark was the action man and I was destined to cheer him on from the sidelines. Of course, there was no arguing with him, and I knew it was because he wanted his family all around him rather than being apart every Sunday afternoon. So after that, Alix and I would take the bikes along the towpath while Tori and Mark were rowing up and down. At least we were together in some way.

Alix was braking right in front of me, and I almost skidded off the track into the bank because I'd been miles away. A shout from the water made us both turn as we slid off our saddles and our bikes came to a standstill. Mark's boat was skimming past in a flash of oars which cut into the water with barely a splash.

As I watched him pulling on the oars and staring straight ahead, I could hardly believe that he was going to be based at home with us for the next two years. We'd spent the last couple of years with so much separation while he'd been commuting to Catterick for a few months and was then deployed to Iraq for another six. The regiment was based at Ballykilner, and although more operations were on the horizon, I would try not to think about that for the moment. Right now he was here and we were a family again.

A few minutes later, as were leaning our bikes against the posts beside the café, we heard the splash of oars again and Tori's boat slinked past, but not quite as fast as the one ahead. We stood and waved and shouted encouragement, then Alix took my hand and we headed up the steps to the café.

"We'll have to be quick, or we'll miss Daddy coming back down." I could see she didn't want to let him out of her sight. She probably thought he was about to disappear again if she didn't keep a close eye on him.

*"His sage advice was always on the money
and we loved the way he put his arms around
those having a harder time of it."*

Major (now Lieutenant Colonel) Darren Denning

CHAPTER 14

July 2009: Dromara

... a time to be still

Mark had been back from Afghanistan for a couple of days. He didn't know I was watching as he spun the wheel of the upturned bike and then stopped it quickly with his hand, before leaning down to make a minute adjustment at the centre of the wheel with a spanner. Various bike tools, cloths, and bottles of oil and lubricant were scattered on the drive. He picked up an oil-stained cloth to wipe his hands and paused as he looked down at his palms. I wondered what he was thinking. *What can he see in his hands?* His face looked serious, but almost frightened. He reached up to wipe away the perspiration on his forehead and looked up as Alix appeared beside him. She was so pleased her dad was working on her bike. She was becoming more confident on it, but it was only a few weeks since the stabilizers had come off.

Through the open window I could hear her asking, "Did you fix it, Daddy?" Alix was smiling at him, her small hands holding the handlebars of an aluminium scooter.

As I watched him reach out to stroke her soft cheeks, I felt a lump in my throat and tears sprang into my eyes. He was talking more quietly now, but I knew he was saying something about oiling the bike and was pointing out something by the chain. I knew he was trying to look stern and bit my lip. *I love this man so much*, I thought.

Alix grinned and then, shrugging her shoulders, turned to scoot off toward the road. Pausing halfway down the drive, she called back to him, "You don't really need to show me, Daddy. Tori knows. She'll do it for me!"

I opened the window wider and said, "Mark, how long are you gonna be? I've made coffee – do you want it out there?"

He looked up and nodded.

A few minutes later I walked toward him, a steaming mug in my hand.

"You're looking sexy, Mrs Hale," he said. I bent down and kissed him, while he ran his hand up the leg of my skinny jeans.

"Mark, behave!" I said, laughing, and stepped away from him. "What are you cooking? Smells good."

"Roast beef and Yorkshires. You approve?" He smiled and then a shadow flickered across his face. I saw it. "What? What's the matter? What are you thinking?"

"I... nothing."

"Tell me. It is something... What is it?"

He had stopped looking at me and was gazing down at the mess of cloths and tools on the drive. "I was just thinking about the last time you cooked roast beef with all the lads before we deployed. It was a great night."

I nodded. I remembered it too: the laughter, the massive joint of silverside, the wine, and the jokes. It had been a bit of a last supper for them all. They were all looking forward to going to Afghanistan and the challenges it would hold. It was what they had trained for. They were excited in some ways, but apprehensive at the same time.

I knew we were both thinking about Paul Mervis, who had been part of the party that night. Lt Paul Mervis had been killed early in the tour. I had read about it later, how he had been on foot patrol with eight soldiers in front of him. He was the ninth person to pass by a hidden IED, and when it blew, he was killed.

My voice was slightly shaky. "Why didn't you tell me about Paul at the time?"

Mark looked up at me, then turned his gaze away toward the road. "I couldn't... I didn't want to talk about it," he said.

I could feel my heart pounding, as if I were walking on a minefield that could blow at any moment. Mark usually told me everything. *Why is this tour so different?* I wondered. He turned back to the bike and it was obvious he didn't want to say any more.

So I just said, "Don't let your coffee go cold," and went back in to turn the meat.

* * *

This is happiness, I thought, as I let out a deep sigh of contentment and wriggled myself further down the bed, nestling my head just below his shoulder and kissing his skin softly. *Three days. He's been home three days.* Earlier that day we'd enjoyed our first Sunday roast together as a family since his return. It had been so special, and I wanted those days to last forever. I could feel his heart pounding below my head and I reached across and laid my hand gently on his chest. His body trembled briefly under my touch and I lifted my head to look at him. His eyes had flicked open, but he wasn't looking at me: they were fixed straight ahead at a spot on the opposite wall.

"Honey," I whispered, hardly daring to break the silence of his blank gaze. He didn't move. His body suddenly felt clammy and cool against my hand. I sat up, feeling frightened. "Mark, Mark!" I was shaking him now and I could feel panic rising inside me. He dragged his eyes back toward me, as if in slow motion, and laid a hand on one of mine, which was gripping his arm.

"It's OK, Brenda. It's OK, I'm here."

I took a deep breath. "But you weren't, Mark, you were somewhere else."

I sighed, sinking back onto the pillows beside him, and then turned onto my side to look at him. "We've done this before, right, Mark? We know how to cope with a tour. We'll be alright, won't we?" I couldn't help looking for reassurance. "It's just a tour, like any other."

He held my gaze now and spoke softly. "Afghan is completely different, Brenda."

Suddenly I thought he looked vulnerable, and I could see something I'd never seen before deep in his green eyes. But I nodded and swallowed. "It's hard with so many being killed," I said, "but at least with an IED the boys are dying instantly."

His eyes moved away from me and he turned to stare at the wall again. When he turned back, I could see tears slipping down his cheeks. In a choked voice, he said, "Brenda, most of them don't die instantly, and they know they're dying." The tears fell faster now. I reached out and put my arms around him as he buried his head in my chest. I could feel my body being rocked by his stifled sobs as he gasped to gain control. As I stroked his hair gently, he began to talk. "It shouldn't have happened. I can't believe Paul was hit. But there was nothing I could do. I wasn't there. I couldn't protect them. He was so young, Brenda, such a great guy, huge potential. It's not fair. I miss him. Every time I think of him I feel sick. It doesn't seem right."

I let him talk, and we both cried as we remembered our dear friend.

A while later, he wiped the tears from my face with the back of his fingertips and leaned back against the pillows. "We're going to have a lot of trouble after Afghan is finished because this is really playing with the boys' heads." He looked gravely concerned. I could tell he was worried. And this was his area. Studying for his PhD in post-traumatic stress gave him a sharp focus on the mental state of "his boys". So he would have been watching for tell-tale signs, and particularly in those who might have been more vulnerable or not as mentally strong or able to cope with all that was happening around them. As Battle Group Logistics Officer, 2 Rifles, Mark was in charge of everything from toilet rolls to bullets, from water to helicopter supplies, and he was also the TRiM officer (Trauma Risk in Management). That meant being there for any of them who needed to talk.

Mark had cried before. He cried every time he left the girls and me. But never, ever in the twenty-four years I had known him had I seen him cry over his guys at work. I lay back against him, and this time he was stroking my hair. "I'm sorry about all that; it's been hard out there..." He paused. "How are you doing, Brenda?"

I could feel a cauldron of bubbling emotions stirring beneath the surface and I took a breath, intending to talk calmly and factually about what had been happening. "It's been a horrific tour and it's really hard trying to protect the children. Not letting them watch the news, turning off the radio when items come up. I want to listen, but I can't in case it upsets them."

Suddenly I was feeling angry about the stress of the last few months. I sat up and turned toward him. "What about us at home? Do you know how difficult it is for the wives left at home, trying to keep things on an even keel? Not letting the children get worried. When you hear someone is killed, you hold your breath and then you feel relieved that it's not your husband in one second, then immediately you feel incredibly guilty. I've been living a nightmare, frightened each day when I don't hear from you that something has happened. You haven't a clue, Mark. And who is looking after the wives and their mental welfare?" I knew my voice was angry and tears were brimming in my eyes, but I couldn't help it.

Mark stayed silent and played with my hair. I looked across at him. "You've 'trimmed' me, haven't you?" He nodded slowly and I smiled at him through my tears, knowing I would burst with love for him. It was his job to let the boys talk to him after being out on patrol or when a mate was injured or killed. He knew it was important to get the anger and the emotions out, to let people talk.

As he drew his arms around me more tightly, I pulled away slightly and looked at him more sternly. "And who's trimming you, Mark? Who's looking after your mental welfare?"

He tried not to smile. "When I get to Oz, I'll take the bikes with Andy and we'll go away for a couple of days." I knew that was his way and I stopped resisting his arms, and relaxed back into the security of his warm chest and beating heart. He felt so alive.

*"In a difficult place, in difficult times,
he was an anchor point to many."*

Major (now Lieutenant Colonel) Darren Denning

CHAPTER 15

July 2009

... a time to laugh

Sand was spattering in all directions as Alix banged the spade on the back of the red bucket. She was smacking it quite hard, almost angrily. "Alix!" I said, brushing clumps of wet sand off the picnic blanket. "It's going everywhere – be more careful."

She grinned and then glanced back down toward the water, where deep blue waves were tumbling onto the shore. Clusters of black figures were dotted among the crumbling white foam, brightly coloured boards clasped against them being buffeted and bounced in the surf. I followed her gaze, searching for two particular figures in wetsuits. "I can't see them. Can you?" I asked.

She shook her head and turned back to the red bucket. Gripping her hands around the rim at the bottom, she looked up at me. "Will it work this time?"

I shuffled across on the blanket toward the growing pile of fresh sand, a graveyard of failed sandcastle attempts. "Slowly, you have to lift it slowly," I said, holding my breath as I watched her, and willing it to stay together. If it didn't work, I knew her frustration would grow and she'd want to be back out in the waves with her sister and her dad. She was so skinny, she couldn't take long in the cold water before her hands started to turn blue. Even on a sunny day, it took me a long time to warm her up after an hour in the freezing North Atlantic.

The red bucket eased off slowly and an almost perfect sand turret emerged, with just the tiniest section of crumbling at one side. Her eyes focused unhappily on the crumbled edge and she shook her head. "Still too dry... we need more wet sand, Mummy." She jumped to her feet, snatching up the empty bucket. "Come on, let's go to the water; the sand's better down there." She held out her hand to me.

Down at the water's edge, the crash of waves was even louder and I watched Alix running in and out of the shallow water before it was sucked back out by the next breath of sea. She was wearing a pair of knee-length denim shorts and a bright green sweatshirt with a hood. For a moment she stood still, her ankles washed by the water, the bucket dangling from one hand and the spade in the other. She was staring out into the distant waves, and then she pointed. "There they are," she said, and then she began jumping up and down. "Dad's caught a big wave – see, see?"

She looked back at me for a second and I followed her gaze. I could see him now, his hands gripping the edge of the board, his dark hair just visible above the froth, and his unmistakeable grin. As the board slowed into the shallows he stood up and waved in our direction, before turning and wading out through the walls of waves that were now breaking against his chest. I wanted to freeze these precious moments, to stop time and just enjoy being together without any worries. I tried to crush the nagging thoughts about his return next week.

Alix was filling her bucket again, further back from the waves. "I'm going to build it here, by the wet sand," she called across.

"They'll see it when they come in." And she continued banging the bottom of the bucket, before sliding out a perfectly shaped mould.

The castle was taking shape, but before it was complete, Tori and Mark emerged dripping and laughing from the sea. "Hey! Great castle, Alix." Tori stood admiring the semicircle of neat casts, and her sister beamed back at her.

Mark dropped his board and knelt down beside the partially built sandcastle. "Not sure these are lined up properly, Alix." His eyes were trained on the gaps between the towers. "The enemy could squeeze through here and then we'll be overrun."

She tipped her head on one side while Tori chuckled quietly. "That's your job, to fill in the gaps. And I can't do the one in the middle either – I can't reach."

Their dark and blonde heads were close together as Mark listened to Alix's instructions while she filled another bucket.

"Is there any hot chocolate, Mum?" Tori was shivering, even in her wetsuit, but I could see she was keen to help with the castle.

I nodded. "I'll go and get it, and your towels. You look freezing."

She shook her head and pushed her wild curly hair away from her face. "The water wasn't cold, was it, Dad? The waves were epic."

A few hours later, the sea at our backs, we trundled up from the beach, laden with bags, blankets, wetsuits, and boards. Partway up the path through the dunes, I stopped and looked back at the arc of golden sand, the rock-edged cliffs, and a shimmering blue sea trimmed with rows of white lace waves. I wished I'd taken my camera. As I let out a sigh, I felt Mark's arm slide around my shoulder. "We're going to have to live somewhere like this one day, Bren."

"I wish... Such an amazing view. We must bring the camera down tomorrow."

He pressed his lips against my hair, and then ruffled it playfully with his hand. "Come on, then. I'll take this." He heaved the bulging bag over his back as if it were weightless, wetsuits and body boards jammed under his other tanned arm. I followed, sinking my bare feet into his deep footprints, hugging a bundle of damp towels against my chest and willing thoughts of next week to disappear.

"Who fancies an ice cream?" he called out as we caught up with the girls, who were dragging their boards up the path by the cords.

* * *

A narrow trail of melted ice cream was sliding down the side of the cone toward Alix's hand. Her sand-caked legs dangled a few inches from the ground where she was sitting on a low stone wall opposite the ice cream shack, where a young couple where waiting patiently – the last of a small queue to be served.

Just as I was about to say something, Mark leaned forward and ran his tongue up the cone, scooping up the melting mass.

"Dad…" Tori protested, but Alix barely noticed and continued licking the soft ice cream, which was also now smeared around the sides of her mouth and top lip. I don't like mess, but beach holidays were like that, with sand, squashed sandwiches and damp towels, ice cream smears on their clothes, and sweet wrappers and crisps in every corner of the car. While we were on holiday, I did my best to ignore the messiness, although I couldn't wait to get them into the shower at the cottage. Mark knew I'd been staring at the cone and he gazed across at me now, winking as he said, "You enjoying that, Alix?"

She looked up at us all, a blob of white ice cream now spattered on the end of her nose. We all started giggling. She looked like Coco the Clown, with huge white lips and a bobbly nose. Tori was convulsed with laughter, almost choking on her cornet. "Alix, stop it…" she said, between bursts of coughing and laughter.

I couldn't bear it any more so I pulled out a tissue and started dabbing her nose and cheeks. "Anyone would think it was face paint, not ice cream," I muttered.

* * *

"It's not here, Mummy. I can't find it. Have you seen it?"

I sighed as I began to stack the breakfast dishes away, and then called back up the stairs, "Where did you have it last?" Then I muttered to myself, "Why am I supposed to know exactly where everything is anyway?"

I heard Tori stomping down the stairs. "I had it on the way here in the car…"

"Well, look in the car, then…" I carried the pile of plates through to the kitchen as she was brushing past me to the back door. "It's probably locked, Tori. Hang on, I'll get the keys."

I rummaged through my handbag. Among the jumble of bits and pieces, my phone fell out onto the worktop with the keys. I glanced down at the screen and noticed some missed calls. It was Mark's mother, Dianne. The phone signal where we were was very patchy. I picked it up and went back into the lounge, wondering where the signal would be strongest. Mark appeared in the doorway with a bundle of wetsuits in his arms, just as my phone started ringing.

"Hi, Dianne," I said. "I've just seen you called…"

She interrupted me and asked if we'd seen the news.

"No, well, actually the TV reception's not great here. What is it?"

"Mark should look at the news. Something else has happened."

I looked across at Mark, who was watching me from the other

side of the room. I put my hand over the phone and said, "It's your mum. She says we need to check the news."

He went to the TV and turned it on. Seconds later his phone started ringing. Putting it to his ear, his face began to drain of colour. I could see him nodding and asking questions. "Which company? What else do we know?"

He'd gone into military mode. He moved toward the stairs and began to make another phone call, but he turned back briefly and said, "There's been another incident. Five soldiers. They were ours."

My heart sank. I reached out my hand to him, but he was already turning away.

Tori appeared in the doorway waving a small leather bag. "Under the seat all the..." She paused. "What? What's the matter? What's happened?"

I sank down onto an armchair in front of the TV and picked up the remote. Eventually a local news channel flashed on. A scene of trucks in the desert flicked onto the screen. There was a reporter speaking to the camera. I could just make out some of the words: "Five more British soldiers... the latest casualties..."

"Where's Dad?" Tori asked.

"I think he's upstairs making a call."

It was a bad start to the day. When Mark came back down, his face looked set and distant. I knew in his head he was back in Afghanistan.

Part of me didn't want to ask as we all sat looking at him. "Did you get through? Is there more news?"

"I don't know much, but five were involved and it was 2 Rifles and... they weren't clear about which company. Darren's going to call me back."

Sitting on the arm of a chair, he went deadly still, his eyes trained on the TV footage of a truck and a damaged building.

The words of the report seemed to echo round the room: "Five soldiers in the same incident, part of 2nd Battalion, The Rifles." It was as if a damp blanket of death had descended on the holiday and I didn't know how we would shake it off.

It took a bit longer to get to the beach and I was glad of the roar of the surf to drown out all the other thoughts in my head. Alix was engrossed in digging a hole, and Mark and Tori had been out in the surf for half an hour or so, when Mark suddenly appeared in front of us. He was looking at Alix and had a mischievous smile on his face.

"Come on, Alix." She looked up. "You're coming in with me and you're going to catch a wave," he said.

She looked delighted, if a little wary. I jumped up to follow, grabbing a towel and hoping he wasn't going to give her hypothermia.

I stood in the shallows as they ploughed out through the surf. Sometimes Alix would get pushed back, but he would be there to pull her forward, reaching down with his strong arms to take her into the deeper water, further from the breakers. With so many bobbing bodies in black wetsuits in the water it was hard to spot them sometimes. But then I saw Alix tumbling through, trying to grasp her board as it flew up into the air, tossed about by the power of a particularly large roller. I bit my lip. *She's getting cold. I bet she can hardly grip the board.*

Tori appeared further up the beach and jogged through the shallow water toward me, her board under her arm. "Alix is doing well. She nearly caught a wave just then – did you see?"

"I know she's doing great... but the wind's cold."

We turned to watch them. Mark was pointing back out to sea and I could see a bulge building in the water. It looked like quite a big wave and it was almost on top of them. Alix was kicking her feet, her arms stretched out to the board in front.

She looked so tiny. Suddenly she was engulfed in the wave, but then she was almost on top of it, her board pressed beneath her as the power of the surf pushed her forward. She sped toward the shore, wobbling slightly from side to side. Seconds later she was a few feet away and standing up, the board still in her hands. Mark came splashing in behind her and swept her up in his arms, swinging her round. "You did it!" he said. "You caught your first wave, Alix!"

She was jumping up and down and then hugging him and I was clapping. Tori grabbed her hand.

"Come on, let's go again!"

They charged off. Mark and I looked at each other and there was a shared joy and pride between us. For a brief moment the news had been forgotten. We were just a family on holiday again.

* * *

The mood over our meal that night was more subdued. *We're all tired,* I thought. But deep down I knew this was affecting him more than he would say. Later as I leaned against him on the settee, when the girls were both in bed, I thought about our first day on the beach. It had been so windy and a perfect day for the power kites. The girls had run after him as he was pulled along the sand and they'd taken turns to have a go themselves. They'd been falling over, and little Alix was dragged several feet before Mark came to the rescue. Then they'd fallen in a heap together, laughing. I could picture his face beaming at me after one really fast gust had almost lifted him off the ground. That night we'd had steak and potato wedges. He'd opened a bottle of wine and we'd toasted the house in France we would buy one day. We were already thinking ahead to our life after the army in a few years' time and beginning to make plans. We also talked about the trip to Australia to see Andy and Kathy at Christmas for his "post op" leave – we were all set and the flights were booked for the big adventure. The future was bright. We just had to get this tour finished. Today's news had brought that home to me like a slap in the face.

Neither of us slept well, and when I woke up, the space beside me felt cold and empty. I pulled on a top and my PJs and found him sitting by the TV downstairs, with the sound on low. I knew something else had happened from the way he was looking at me. "What now?" I asked. I could hear the exasperation in my own voice.

He didn't meet my eyes; he just kept looking at the images on the screen, the same news channel. "Apparently two Russian helicopters have been shot down."

I breathed a sigh of relief. "Thank God not our lads then..." Then I corrected myself. "But yes, awful, still awful."

A heavy silence hung between us. I knew there was something else he wasn't saying. I waited. Then when he didn't say anything, I asked him if he wanted a cup of tea. It felt easier to be busy doing something in the kitchen.

When I carried in the mugs I could see the early morning sun lighting up patches on the hazy cliffs in the distance. I moved toward the window, both hands cradling the mug of tea. It was so beautiful; the sea was a flat calm, almost like a lake. The sun's rays were dancing across the water, making it glisten and sparkle like a bed of diamonds. I turned back toward Mark and would have asked him to come and see, but a mask had fallen across his face again, and he was deep in thought. He was somewhere else. I moved round and sat on the chair nearest to him. I wanted to give him space to say what was on his mind.

He sipped his tea slowly and, putting the mug down beside him, he eventually found the words he needed to explain. "It's bad, Brenda, these helicopters going down..." I kept my eyes on his. "They supply the FOBs [Forward Operating Bases], so that means the boys won't be getting supplies so easily. It's going to affect them badly. Those supplies are a lifeline. It's what keeps them going when everything else is so... so awful. I should be there. I should be out there with them. I know what needs to be done."

I knew why he felt like that, but I wanted to argue, to say we needed him here too and he needed a break as much as anyone. I wanted to say, "Don't ruin the time we've got by wishing you were back there." I bit my lip and looked into the mug for inspiration.

He had already told me he was worried about the mental state of "his boys" and that the tour was "messing with their heads". I knew they looked up to him; to some of them he was almost a father figure. Mark was forty-two. He was an older soldier. He'd started in the ranks and worked his way up. He was highly respected. He'd told me they used to say, "Boss, can you come out with us? Because if you're out with us, we'll be safe."

The previous evening, he'd told me he would say in response, "You know your drills. You're well trained."

Then they would say, "If you come out with us, your God will be out there with us."

Mark would tell them, "He's your God too. You just need to ask Him and He'll be with you too."

I wanted to say something about God looking after people and how we would pray for them and for the families of those who'd just been killed. But the words died in my throat and I took another sip of tea instead. A voice inside my head was asking, "Are my prayers enough to protect Mark when he goes back? Why would God protect Mark and not those other poor people?"

Mark reached his hand across and laid it on my knee. "I'm sorry, Bren, I know this isn't easy for you." He hesitated, and his focus was dragged back to the images on the screen. Almost to himself, he said, "If I can just get back and make sure they're doing everything they should. They can't afford to get careless... a lot of them are just kids. They're so young."

I prayed my own prayer then, a silent prayer, that I would be patient and not get angry with him, because now he was disappearing from us, even before his leave was over.

"Big in stature, both physically and in terms of personality, he was utterly unflappable and always dismissed any pressure or difficulty with his easy sense of humour and calming presence."

Major (now Colonel) Karl Hickman

CHAPTER 16

July 2009

... a time to leave

Tarragon chicken was one of Mark's favourites, so that's what I'd cooked on his last night at home. Everything had been different about this leave. Mark would usually have gone out on his bike and gone down to the rowing club. But not this time. When I'd asked him if he was going out for a ride, he'd shaken his head and said, "I need to spend every moment with you guys... I don't want to waste a minute." That had surprised and unnerved me at the same time. It made me realize how much he missed us and how this time back home was so precious. He had pottered around the house and tinkered with his bikes. He did do some weights in the garage and he'd taken his new bike off to get something fixed, but not for long.

I closed the dishwasher and went back into the lounge and glanced at the clock. "It's time for bed, Alix."

She was snuggled up on Mark's lap. A few minutes later, he stood up while she wrapped her arms around his neck, hanging from him like a monkey. "Are you excited about the film tomorrow?" I asked, trying to chase away the thoughts of goodbyes. She nodded vigorously and hugged Mark even tighter. "So who's taking you to bed tonight?" She smiled sweetly and looked up at Mark. We both smiled and I reached up to kiss her on the cheek, whispering, "Sweet dreams, darling."

Mark carried her upstairs. Five minutes later, when I went up to empty the bathwater, I could hear him reading to her. It was his regular routine; he'd been going through her Children's Bible for the last few days. It was the second time he'd read the Bible to her. I stood by the bedroom doorway and watched him leaning in close; her hands were clasped together and her eyes tightly shut. I could hear him praying softly and then they both began speaking together, "Our Father, who art in heaven..." Tears sprang to my eyes; I couldn't help it. Seeing them together like that was always moving. I brushed my eyes, annoyed with myself for getting upset.

* * *

Thursday came, as it always does – there was no stopping it. When I opened my eyes that morning, I closed them again immediately. I didn't want to go through it all again – watching him pack up his rucksack, that painful journey to the barracks, all of us feeling sick inside. I rolled onto my side and slid my arm across his stomach, my head resting on his chest. "I wish this wasn't happening, Mark."

"I know... but it will be OK... It's going to be OK, Brenda."

His voice had a slight catch in it which made me realize his emotions were only just being held in check. He ran his hand through my hair and pulled me closer, with his arms wrapped tightly around me. A quiet voice from the landing was being shushed, and seconds later there was a tap on the door and Alix wandered in, followed by Tori. They clambered up onto the bed, as Mark and I eased ourselves upright against the pillows.

"Where's my breakfast in bed, then?" he asked.

They shook their heads and Alix nudged her sister in the ribs.

"What time are you going?" asked Tori.

"Ages yet," said Mark. "Come on, I need girly hugs!"

They both dived toward him and he wrapped his arms around them, squeezing so hard that they started to laugh and squeal.

* * *

The queue didn't seem to be getting any shorter and my legs were tired. It had been a difficult day, although I wasn't in any hurry for it to end. I'd have been happy if the next day never came, because that would mean Mark wouldn't be going back.

There was a babble of conversation and excited chatter among all the children on either side of us. Many were dressed in black capes and others had fluffy toy owls clasped under their arms. We'd chosen the afternoon showing, but it was still packed. The latest Harry Potter film – *Harry Potter and the Half-Blood Prince* – was still a sell-out even though it had been running for a few days. Alix was beside herself with excitement, hopping from one foot to the other and explaining breathlessly to Mark what had happened at the end of the last film. Tori yawned. She was trying to look less interested, but I knew she was mad keen to see the next instalment too.

"Who do you like best, Alix?" Tori questioned. "Harry or Ron?"

Alix raised her eyebrows. "Harry, of course... I don't know why you'd even ask!"

"But Ron is funnier," Tori explained. "And I think he's much hotter than Harry. No wonder Hermione prefers him."

"No, no, that's not true."

The debate continued. I caught Mark's eye across the top of Alix's head. He reached round and took my hand and I felt him squeeze it gently. Nothing was said but we both knew what the other was thinking. There were only a few hours left of this special time with family before we would be pulled apart again. I kept telling myself we were on the countdown to him coming back permanently. Because he'd taken his R&R in the second half of the tour, he had already done sixteen and a half weeks. He only had another fourteen left when he returned. We'd broken the back of it, and yet I couldn't relax. I knew we weren't home and dry yet.

Later that evening, after Harry and his friends had escaped near death again at the hands of an increasingly powerful Voldemort, we were all emotionally exhausted. I'd held Mark's hand all through the film, and in some ways it had been good to be together in the dark, not looking at the expression on each other's faces. That morning we had found it hard to make eye contact; we were trying not to show the girls how anxious we both were. It was completely unlike Mark. I knew he just wanted to be Daddy while he was at home, and not a soldier, but it was hard because while he was home people out there were still dying. Despite the undercurrent of fear between us, we tried to make it routine, as if this was what Daddy always did: he went away and came back again.

* * *

The car crunched to a halt outside the low brick building. A muscle in Mark's cheek seemed to twitch, but his face was almost expressionless. I knew he was preparing himself to go back into army mode. He was Captain Hale now. He had been for the last few hours as he'd started to get his head back into the operation. Perhaps it had never really left. His hands were still gripping the steering wheel and he turned to look at me for a moment before he pulled open the door. I forced myself to get out and moved toward the back of the car while he was kissing the girls goodbye. I put my hand out against the warm metal of the car to steady my trembling legs. I'd been feeling sick all morning and my stomach was still churning like a washing machine. *We have to get this over*, I said to myself.

Mark appeared beside me and I was enveloped in his arms. It was a huge, powerful hug and then we kissed. It was a kiss that lasted a long time and we broke away breathless. My cheeks were wet with tears and I could see there were tears in his eyes too. He yanked out his rucksack and slung it over one shoulder, slamming the boot down. "I'll email you as soon as I get to Bastion," he said.

I tried to control the tremble in my voice. "OK, safe flight."

I watched him walk toward the building. The coach was coming later to pick them all up, but Mark had said he wanted to do some paperwork before it arrived. As I drove off, I could see him standing there. I looked in the mirror and watched him wave at us before he walked into his office. I knew he would want to get himself together before he saw all the guys.

"He was always there when you needed him, putting others first and ensuring the success of the mission."

Major (now Colonel) Karl Hickman

CHAPTER 17

August 2009

... a time to hope

I sniffed the rich, nutty, slightly alcoholic aroma drifting up from the odd assortment of items spread out on the table. *I hope the postman doesn't try and eat this. It smells so good*, I thought, as I finished sealing down the foil around a small dark fruit cake.

"I hope your daddy appreciates this," I said, speaking half to myself and half to Alix. She was equally preoccupied at the other end of the table, adding elaborate floral decorations to a carefully written letter. She glanced across at the assorted heap of goodies with a puzzled expression. "Will all those things really fit into that box?"

I sighed and smiled. "The amount of times I've done this, I should know what fits in! Anyway, get on with that letter. I want to get it all packed and off to the Post Office this afternoon." I slid the foil parcel into a plastic bag and began carefully loading items into the paper-lined shoe box, turning them around to fit the odd shapes into one another like a 3D puzzle. The box of Earl Grey tea bags was loaded next to the cake parcel, and some of Mark's favourite shower gel, sealed in another plastic bag, was jammed in beside a rolled-up *Cycling Weekly*. Finally, I picked up the last item on the table – a small, white envelope. I held it to my lips and closed my eyes, kissing it softly at the seal before laying it on the top of the box of goodies.

Glancing up, I saw Alix watching me. Neither of us spoke, but an unsaid sadness hung in the air. I slid an empty white envelope along the table toward her. "This is for yours," I said.

Alix nodded and bent her head, returning her concentration to the green leaves of a red-petalled flower.

Later that evening I checked my emails again. Sitting in one of the huge cream-coloured sofas, I sank back against the cushions and clicked on a new message.

What colour tonight, Mark? What I wouldn't give to know he'd be coming home in a day or two, I thought. I looked across at the card with the teddy climbing out of a basket that was propped against the base of the lamp. Picking it up, I scanned through the words again.

> *Honey*
>
> *Just a wee card to remind you that I love and miss you very much.*
>
> *You are very much at the centre of my life, just as you have been since that very first night we met. I can never imagine a life without you, our marriage seems so natural. It was definitely meant to be, you are my every thought and every breath.*
>
> *Thank you for blessing my life with fullness, joy, and happiness.*

My life is blessed by you too, I whispered.

The second half of the tour seemed to be passing so slowly. Of course, he shouldn't have been there at all. His next posting had been confirmed and he should have started it in July, but Mark had a job to do and wouldn't leave the tour early. "They need me, Brenda. I need to be there to check they are doing things right," he'd said, as I'd tried to persuade him to cut short and take up the posting. He had an intense sense of responsibility for the safety of "his boys". Every injury, every death, felt like a body blow and made him renew his determination to make the lads rigorous in their safety drills, and to check and double check each other every time they stepped out on patrol.

Still, it's only ten more weeks. They've done twenty-two and this is the home straight. We should be able to relax a bit. But I couldn't. Each day I woke with a familiar knot in my stomach, thinking, *Will there be an email? Has something happened?* The dread of hearing the morning news bulletins followed.

I shivered. *Stop being morbid, Brenda,* I thought. *We have two years in Lisburn to look forward to – be cheerful!* I scrolled through the colour options on the email and chose a carefree pink with some elaborate font, just for fun. *This will make him smile,* I thought, as I began yet another letter to "My darling Mark".

* * *

The road was jammed with cars which had stopped haphazardly as doors were flung open and excited children, carrying knapsacks and lunch boxes, jostled one another to squeeze into a familiar vehicle. I glanced at my watch and checked the rear-view mirror where I could see a large van hovering behind the bumper. The three girls in the back of the car were giggling excitedly.

"At your house? Really?" one them exclaimed.

"Oh, not at my house, it was in the road behind..." Her voice trailed off to a whisper. At the same time a car horn sounded behind me.

"OK, mate," I said. I felt hot and irritated now as I edged the car forward nearer to the one in front, which was still loading up with children. It was a scorching day. I could feel beads of perspiration sliding down my back and I brushed the damp strands of hair away from my forehead.

"Bet you all can't wait to get into that pool," I said, wishing I was going for a swim today as well.

A few minutes later we were drawing into the parking bay beside the offices of the *Banbridge Chronicle*, where Tori was working for a couple of weeks. I could see her leaning on a low wall, intently texting on her phone. I wound down the window and called across to her. She smiled, slid her phone into her pocket, and headed toward the car.

"The traffic's awful today, and we're meant to be at the pool by 4.30 p.m.," I sighed, as I edged the car out into the busy road.

"Aw, chill, Mum, there's loads of time." Tori yawned and stretched her long, jeans-clad legs out in front of her. Then she turned to the girls in the back. "You had a good day, Alix?" There was a burst of laughter and Alix began to recount some of the funniest moments of the day, which mainly related to a particular boy who was the main source of entertainment for the summer school.

The shrill ring of my phone interrupted the laughter. Glancing down, I saw it was a blocked number calling. Keeping my eyes on the road in front, I snatched it up and handed it to Tori. "It might be your dad, Tori, you take it."

She looked back at me and nodded, and I put my finger to my lips to let the girls in the back know to be quiet.

"Hi, Dad," she purred happily. "Yer, we're all fine. We're taking Alix swimming, Mum's driving... It was great. I'm loving it..."

A few minutes later, as an empty bus stop loomed, I pulled the car over and Tori handed me the phone. I could just hear his voice, as there was quite a bit of background noise this time.

"Yes, we're fine, all fine. It's really hot here... What?" I laughed. "Well, no not forty-five degrees actually, but hot for Ireland! ... OK, can you phone Sunday?"

"I'm going out later, Brenda, but I should be able to," he said.

I felt the slight hesitation in his voice and I knew what "going out" meant. "Don't go out, Mark, stay in," I said.

"No, staying in is boring," he joked.

We frequently spoke in code, and although he couldn't tell me much, I knew from his emails that elections were coming up, which meant the Taliban would be more aggressive. It was also the beginning of a special exercise: Panther's Claw. I knew they were going on the attack, and most of all I wanted him to be safe. But I also knew Mark, and I knew he would want to be out there.

Ignoring his last comment, as he said he had to go, I simply said, "Please stay in. I more than love you. Speak to you on Sunday."

*"For no one else does the phrase
'Soldier First' fit better."*

Lieutenant Hannah Keenan

CHAPTER 18

Thursday 13 August 2009

... a time to die

Bright shafts of sunlight were streaming in between the gap in the curtains, shedding gentle white lines across the wooden floor. It was another clear summer's day and I looked at the clock by the bed. Although it was the school holidays, both girls had to be up and out soon. I stretched my legs across the smooth white sheets and, moving my arm to the side, I could feel the empty space where Mark should be.

It's 7 a.m., I thought. *That's 10.30 a.m. there. He might have sent an email.*

Reaching across to the chair beside the bed, I flipped open the laptop and waited as the emails streamed in. Nothing. I felt my heart flutter and then there was that sinking feeling of dread again, deep down in my stomach. Throwing back the sheets, I headed downstairs and went straight to the television to check the BBC news service CEEFAX. I knew if there had been an incident it would be on there. Nothing again. I knew what it meant – there had probably been an incident and there was a communications shutdown.

Mark had explained all this to me before. He always sent an email every day. He would do it every morning and night just to say "Busy today", or 'How are you? I love you", "I miss you", or sometimes just thanking me for a parcel he'd received. But if there was no email it probably meant there had been a communications shutdown, which was called "Op Minimize" in army speak. Whenever a soldier was injured or killed, the phone and email system was shut down until the family had been informed, as they didn't want the news leaking out before next of kin were told.

It had happened more times than I wanted to remember already on this tour. The summer of 2009 was the most difficult tour of Afghanistan the army had faced so far. Mark's regiment – 2 Rifles – were losing men almost on a daily basis, suffering horrific deaths or catastrophic life-changing injuries. I had gone through it many times in the last few months, with increasing frequency, and each time I feared that knock at the door. I had felt that heart-stopping fear and panic that snapped at my heels like a stray dog until the phone rang and I heard his voice. "I'm OK, Brenda, it was Paul, it was Mac, it was Toge…" Their names punched me in the face, then came the guilty relief that it wasn't my Mark. *It wasn't us. Oh, thank You, God, thank You, thank You,* I would say to myself.

Making myself busy in the kitchen, I rehearsed the usual mantra in my head. *I know what this is. I need to be calm. He will email later. It will be OK.*

"Oh, please email me later, honey," I said aloud.

I placed the cereal packets on the table and poured steaming water over the coffee as I attempted to calm my breathing. Steadying the mug in my quivering hand, I headed back upstairs, calling out to rouse the sleeping girls.

Later that morning the supermarket was quiet and I meandered through the aisles, absentmindedly loading items into the trolley. I knew I should have made a list, but I couldn't stop thinking about my emails. I found myself staring at the vast array of packets of tea, wondering where Mark kept all the tea I kept sending. I could picture his tanned smiling face, his deep-set green eyes, creased around the edges as that irrepressible broad grin split across his face. *Wherever you are, honey, be safe*, I whispered to myself, in what was almost a prayer. I didn't want to go home yet, but I suddenly decided I'd had enough of shopping. Without looking up I launched the trolley forward decisively, almost ploughing down a shocked old lady who was trying to cut across to the tea section. Apologizing profusely, I rapidly collected a few more essentials and focused on what to cook for tea.

As I hauled the bags into the car, I decided to call and see my sister on the way home. I told myself there was bound to be a message waiting by the time I got back.

A few hours later I swung the car around the corner of the road and into the drive. I half registered that there was a strange car I hadn't seen before parked further down the street. But I told myself not to be paranoid and that there was bound to be an email when I got in. Heaping the heavy bags of shopping onto the kitchen table, I checked the clock on the wall. It was noon. *Surely there'll be something now*, I thought. But I hesitated. Seeing the breakfast dishes scattered on the table I began clearing them away methodically, loading them into the dishwasher. Each knife and spoon made a clatter as I dropped it into the cutlery holder. I knew I was just trying to give him some more time.

Closing the dishwasher I flipped open the laptop again and found I was holding my breath. There was nothing. Taking a deep breath, I opened up the carrier bags and started to stack butter and vegetables into the fridge. Each time I finished putting a few items in, I turned back to the table and clicked "Send and receive" on the laptop. I could feel my heart beginning to beat more rapidly as I thought about what might be. *Oh God, please let him phone. I'll send him another email*, I whispered to myself. Leaning over the laptop I drew up another message and typed rapidly, "Mark, honey, I'm so worried. Email as soon as you get a chance. I love you so, so much." I held my breath again as I pressed the "Send" button, but over the whoosh of the email being sent, a sudden rap on the front door made me freeze.

In that instant, I could feel an invisible hand clasp my heart, which was now thumping like a stone against my chest. I turned and walked to the door, my hand held against my chest to calm my beating heart. I couldn't help thinking, *They've come to tell me about Mark*. Dragging back the door, I saw a man in a smart grey suit and a lady standing side by side. The man spoke quietly and flashed a military ID card. "We are from the army," he said. "Are you the wife of Captain Mark James Hale?"

The words hit me like a shot from a gun and I stepped back away from them with a gasp, slamming the door shut in their faces. My teeth began chattering and an icy cold feeling had begun seeping through my body. I was shaking. Steadying myself with one hand against the wall, I forced myself to breathe and my instincts kicked back in. *What am I doing, leaving military personnel standing on my doorstep in Northern Ireland?* I thought. I moved back to the door and opened it again, this time a little wider, allowing them to step inside. One of them put an arm around my shoulder and guided me into the living room.

I felt the woman in a dark suit sink down on the sofa beside me, while the man sat on the edge of a chair opposite. He repeated his previous question calmly, "Are you the wife of Captain Mark James Hale?"

I nodded slowly. "Yes."

The man cleared his throat and said, "He was killed today in Afghanistan."

I just shook my head. "No, no... I spoke to him yesterday. He's phoning me on Sunday... He wasn't going out. Are you sure it's the right one? He was born in Salisbury."

I was glancing from one to the other, desperate for them to be wrong. In my head I was praying, *Oh God, please let this be a mistake.* They both nodded with a sombre expression. And the woman looked me in the eyes and said, "Yes, it is the right one."

Now there was a banging pain in my head and my chest felt tight – but no tears came, just disbelief. I could hear my own voice sounding raspy and dry as I stuttered between my chattering teeth, "Is he really dead? My Mark?"

"He died at ten past nine this morning in Bastion."

There were no more details.

*"He wouldn't ask anyone to do a task
he wasn't willing to do himself,
a fact widely acknowledged by all who knew him
and, as such, sought to
live out the example of Christ."*

Captain (now Major) Rupert Streatfeild

Chapter 19

13 August 2009

... a time to cry

Over the next hour or so I sank into a deep fog of shock.

I was staring blankly at the floor when the army Padre arrived. He sat down carefully in the seat across from me and placed his hands on the knees of his perfectly pressed black trousers. He began to speak gently and said he was sorry to hear about my loss. I couldn't speak, but I let his words flow over me. Suddenly I looked up at him, wondering how he could be talking about my Mark, and I said fiercely, "You didn't know my husband, did you?"

He said he didn't.

At that moment, the television screen in the corner of the room caught my eye. It seemed to have suddenly switched on. I stared at it, hardly believing what I was seeing. It was a pair of open church doors – they were the church doors of my own church – and behind them was a piercingly bright light. I could see Mark in front of the doors, and although there was no sound, I could tell he was trying to tell me something. He was looking directly at me saying, "Sweetie, I need to go now."

I nodded, and then I watched him turn and walk in through the doors. The image faded and was gone. And then finally my tears began to fall. Through my tears, I whispered, "He knew he couldn't go without asking my permission… and God would understand that."

The Padre looked confused, but assured me it would take time. I suddenly felt sorry for him, very aware that this was just one of many such visits he would have made in the last few weeks as the regimental losses continued to be heavy.

* * *

My sister and brother-in-law had gone to fetch Alix, but I knew I had to pick up Tori and tell her the news. Sitting in the passenger seat as my friend Jane drove through the teatime traffic, I stared out of the car window and watched as people went about their normal lives. We slowed down to let a mother with two small children cross in front of us. A boy on a motorbike slid past on the inside lane and sped off with a pitiful squeal of his engine. The scenes and sounds were all the same as yesterday. But this day I knew my life had changed forever, and nothing would ever be the same again. *Everything has changed, but nobody knows and nobody cares*, I thought. *If only I could give Tori a few more hours of normal life before her world collapses too.*

But we arrived outside the newspaper offices a few minutes later, where I immediately saw Tori waiting by a low wall. As I got out of the car, leaving my friend Jane in the driver's seat, Tori looked up and then stopped in her tracks.

"Sweetie, get in the car," I said gently, holding my hand out and walking toward her. Her wild hair was billowing out around her and her wide blue eyes stared at my face – I couldn't hide the grief.

Her hands flew to the sides of her face and she started to

scream, frozen to the spot. "No, no, it should have been me," she wailed. "I want to die; it should have been me."

She too had been waiting for an email from her father that never came.

The horror and pain of the day continued for us both as we waited for Alix to come in from summer school. Every time I had to say he had been killed felt like a fresh body blow. I thought, *I'm in the boxing ring now and I'm on my knees. Don't hit me again because I won't get up.* I didn't want to tell Alix. She was too little and I didn't think I could do it. Telling her made it real again, made me certain it wasn't a dream. Beyond that, I felt responsible for inflicting the most devastating pain on the girls. I had to keep telling myself this was really happening. The nightmare had become a reality and the unthinkable had happened to us.

I looked at Tori as we heard the car on the drive and the click of the latch on the front door. Our eight-year-old ran straight to where I was sitting on the sofa. I could tell she knew something was wrong, as the house was full of strangers. I held her against me for a moment, then, placing my hands on her arms and looking straight into her eyes, I said, "Alix, you know Daddy was in the army…" She nodded, her eyes wide with fear. "Well, they sent him to Afghanistan and he got hurt very badly today, so Jesus took him to heaven."

As soon as it was said, her eyes widened and she looked into my eyes. A terrified expression spread across her face as tears began streaming down my face. Silent tears started to slide down her cheeks and she looked down at her feet, sobbing heavily. Then she looked back up at me and said, "But what about my new school shoes? I have to show him my new shoes…"

"It is his wonderfully warm character that I will remember most, always a big smile on his face. He seemed to almost envelop you with his character and presence – he genuinely had an aura about him."

Lieutenant Colonel (now Major General) Rupert Jones

CHAPTER 20

18 August 2009

... a time to mourn

Objects in the room were moving in and out of focus as my eyes shifted from one to the next. I stared at the leaves of the closed book beside my bed and then I caught sight of the edge of the framed photograph next to it. I could hear a strange clattering noise and I tried to turn my head to see where it was coming from. Everything seemed to have gone into slow motion. I shuffled myself more upright in the bed and caught sight of my reflection in the mirror opposite. My face looked white, my eyes were puffy, and I could see my lips were trembling. Then I realized the noise was coming from me. It was my teeth that were chattering and, as I stared at the closed door, I started to shake. *God, don't let this be happening to me. Please, I can't bear it.*

If I had slept at all I hadn't been aware of it. I felt as if I'd watched all the hours of the night passing slowly by as if I was in a nightmare from which there was no escape. I pictured Mark's face again as I'd seen him, turning to say, "I have to go now, sweetie."

A dry sob caught in my throat and I coughed it away. I was beyond tears, beyond crying. I felt as if I was barely alive. Downstairs, I could hear my old school friend Valerie, who had stayed overnight with us, moving about in the kitchen. *Mark*, I whispered, *Mark, don't leave me.* I wanted to wake up and find this was just an awful dream, like so many dreams I'd already had. I drew my legs up toward my chest and buried my face in my hands.

Somehow I'd been warned about what was ahead. I pictured a haunting dream from years before, before Alix had even been born. I'd been standing at an island in a strange kitchen, chopping vegetables. I could see it now, but it wasn't my kitchen downstairs. Tori was there, and for some reason I knew she was sixteen. There was another child standing beside her. I didn't know if they were a boy or a girl, and Mark wasn't there. We were OK as a unit, but Mark wasn't there, and I knew he wasn't there. He physically wasn't about. I could remember telling Mark about the dream the next morning because it had been so strange. *Could that have been a premonition of things to come?*

I shuddered. *Who knows?* As a Christian I believed that God was in control, so why had He allowed my wonderful, God-fearing husband to be killed? Mark had been telling his soldiers about faith; he'd encouraged them to go to church and, if the Padre couldn't be there, he would step in and even lead the Sunday services. It was something he and the commanding officer took turns to do on occasions. He was always caring for others and had even been rescuing others when he died. Nothing made sense about it, except that death comes to us all one day, without exception. But this was too soon. It was all wrong.

I slid out of bed and pulled on a cardigan that was lying on the chair. Wrapping it around me, I stared out on to the road and could see two or three children playing with a football, but the houses on the other side of the street all had their blinds closed. In keeping with Northern Irish tradition when there is a death in the street, our neighbours had closed their curtains out of respect for Mark. I shivered. Doors were closing and opening downstairs and I could hear footsteps and taps running in the bathroom. Last night Tori and Alix had both come into our bed: we had all needed to hold on to each other. Valerie had stayed in the spare room. She was one of a tight-knit group of friends who had gathered round me immediately, taking care of everything in the house. I barely felt able to move and stumbled back to sit on the bed again. There was a gentle tap on the door and Valerie appeared with a mug of coffee. "The girls are having breakfast."

I nodded and she squeezed my hand. After she'd shut the door behind her, I slid back under the duvet and pulled it over my head, wanting the darkness to block out the terrifying thoughts of life without Mark.

When I had eventually forced myself to dress, I went downstairs and found Valerie had taken care of everything. The girls were in the lounge and I sank down at the table in the kitchen. I couldn't eat anything that Valerie offered and I was vaguely aware of people coming and going. But it felt a bit like watching a play, with props coming on and off and actors in conversation. I wasn't really there; I was watching it all from a distance. One of the girls carried in a casserole dish and put it on the worktop. The doorbell rang again and I heard another friend, Jane, saying firmly, "There's no story here."

Valerie shook her head. "It's the media – they keep calling."

* * *

Sometime during the morning the visiting officer (VO), Captain Vince Mears, arrived. He was dressed in a dark suit. He had been out in Afghanistan with Mark and was back on R&R with his family. He'd been on his way back to Brize Norton to fly out again when he'd been called back to be with us. I later discovered that serving officers weren't usually called into that role, but we were a special case because Mark was a Late Entry Officer living in Northern Ireland. Now Vince would be by our side for the coming weeks and possibly months.

There were forms to sign, and I could tell he was struggling with the news too. He told me Mark had been his boss. I asked again about what had happened and Vince carefully explained what he knew. He told me that Mark and Rifleman Daniel Wild had gone to help an injured soldier, Lance-Bombardier Matthew Hatton, after an IED had gone off. As they were carrying him to the helicopter, another device had been triggered, killing two of them immediately, and fatally injuring Mark. They called it a "daisy chain", where devices are linked together to cause maximum destruction.

I knew Mark loved his guys. When the first IED went off he was safe, he wasn't blown up, but he had taken himself out of a safety area and gone to help. He had put himself on the line. This made me crumble inside when I heard it. I had prayed each day that angels would be around him and would protect his feet. The trouble was that the device had been triggered by another soldier's boot, and Mark had been hit by the blast. They told me he had been taken on the helicopter back to Camp Bastion and had died in the hospital. I knew they would have done all they could to save him, and Mark would have been fighting to stay alive, to come back to us. I tried hard not to dwell on what had happened in that final hour. But somehow I did want to know all the details, so that I could really understand what had gone on out there.

"This is the PAX form, Brenda," Vince explained as he pressed open the sheet of paper on the table. "This will ensure you receive the insurance which Mark took out. You sign here."

He handed me a pen and I tried to grip it, but my hand was shaking so much I couldn't keep it steady. "I... why... where do I sign?" I stuttered.

He pointed to a box at the foot of the page, and as I tried to steady the pen, I felt as if I was signing Mark's death warrant. *If I don't sign this, will he be able to come back? Could it all be a dreadful mistake?* I looked up at Vince and he just nodded gently.

"I just want him back. I want him back home," I said.

"They're bringing him back, Brenda."

My bottom lip was quivering, but I took a deep breath. Vince steadied my trembling hand as I tried to scrawl my name as best I could before pushing the papers away. I didn't care about the insurance. I just wanted my Mark. *How could any amount of money make things better?*

* * *

Sometime later I was sitting in the lounge. The door opened and Valerie ushered in our church minister, Bobby Liddle. His usually beaming face looked grave and he walked across and gripped both my hands in his. As he sat down opposite, I was only vaguely aware of soothing words, to which I nodded or gave brief answers. There was a pause, then he asked, "Brenda, have you thought what you're going to do with Mark?"

"No I haven't, because this shouldn't have happened," I replied. "I'm a Christian wife and I've been praying for my Christian husband in the way the Bible says. God should have listened to me."

I was angry and I couldn't hide it.

Mark had once told me he had had his fortune told at a fair when he was fourteen, just for a laugh. I shuddered at the memory. He'd told me about it not long after we'd met. Whoever it was had said the cards predicted he would join the army and die in a foreign field in his forties and be buried in Ireland. I had told him I might not even know him when he was forty and I didn't believe any of that stuff anyway. My mum's neighbour had also dabbled with a Ouija board and when I was a teenager she had said that I would become well known. I'd laughed that off too. After Mark and I became Christians we'd talked about the prediction and we'd prayed about our past links with spiritual forces that were not from God. We believed our lives were in God's hands and that we shouldn't be afraid of the future; rather we should trust in Him.

The previous evening I'd rung Andy Moreland in Australia to tell him about Mark. I'd forgotten it was the middle of the night there. "They got my Mark," I said.

I heard that audible intake of breath from the man who was one of Mark's oldest and dearest friends. "I'm coming over. I'll be there, Brenda."

I was crying then, crying out to Andy and asking him how God could have let it happen.

He said, "God did it because God is sovereign." Then he told me we couldn't understand everything and we had to leave it with God.

Bobby was gentler with me, but he didn't know us both as well as Andy did. He hadn't even known Mark was in the army, because we'd thought it best to keep quiet about that at church for security reasons. Northern Ireland could still be a dangerous place. Bobby told me there was a double grave available outside the church which had been donated for Mark, and for me when the time came.

I felt a lump rising in my throat and choked back tears, surprised by the generosity of someone I didn't even know. They'd recognized that Mark had laid his life down for his friends and they wanted to acknowledge his sacrifice.

Thinking about the funeral made me realize I wanted someone who really knew us both to lead it. Later I sent a message to our old friend Simon Farmer, an army chaplain who had served with Mark in the D&Ds, and I asked him to call me. I knew Mark and Simon had been messaging each other in the last few weeks.

* * *

There seemed to be a fairly constant stream of people coming in and out of the house, and later, when I escaped up to my room, I pulled a pillow against me and closed my eyes. Mark's face appeared out of the blackness. His eyes were smiling at me. My eyes flicked open and I sat upright. *Where is it?* I pulled open the drawer beside my bed. Lying on top was one of the cards he'd sent, with a gorgeous sunset on the front. I opened it up and the writing began to swim in front of me.

> *Life is so empty without you. I miss your company and your support so much. Roll on R&R and that feeling of togetherness again.*
>
> *Honey, I love you dearly. I always have done and I always will do.*
>
> *Goodbye and God bless.*
> *Yours forever,*
> *xxxx Mark xxxx*

I stared at the words written just a couple of months earlier. *Why did you say "goodbye"?*

Staring into the drawer again, I pushed aside the bits and pieces, feeling underneath for another card that had a bunch of sunflowers on the front. As I drew it out, I had butterflies. Mark loved writing poems and little limericks. He'd done that ever since we'd met, and there were always poems for everyone's birthdays. The previous February, just before he deployed in March, he'd given me a poem on Valentine's Day. They were often funny or even a bit naughty. But this one was different. He was talking about the boys and going to support them and serving Queen and Country. It was such a serious poem. When he gave it to me, I had looked at him and said, "What's this?"

He just held my gaze, his expression inscrutable.

"You're saying goodbye to me. You're saying goodbye, Mark."

"No, you're reading it out of context," he had said. "No, Brenda, it has taken me months of trying to write, having to hide in the loo in the middle of the night, trying to get my thoughts together to write this."

One verse of the poem talked about him not being able to check on the girls when they were sleeping:

No longer there at night, to peep around the door
Or guide you through your trials; until you prosper for sure.

He said he knew we had a lot to achieve and that we were going to go on and achieve it. The final verse made tears spring to my eyes as I read it:

The prospect of this parting has opened the heart
Rekindled these feelings, rarely felt so strongly, since from the start.
Overwhelmed with emotion and tinged with sorrow
My soul will be aching and longing for "tomorrow".

As I let the words seep in, I needed to hear his voice again. I reached for my laptop, powered it up, and scrolled through my emails. It was almost as if he was speaking to me.

"He was 'undentable', and we in 2 RIFLES have invented this new word in honour of Mark. Nothing fazed him, however demanding the situation, and his ability to absorb work, pressure, and other people's worries was genuinely legendary. That is what 'undentable' now means."

Lieutenant Colonel (now Brigadier) Rob Thomson

CHAPTER 21

18 August 2009

... a time to weep

Everything was precision-timed and organized military style. It was comforting to be in the hands of the professionals. Standing on the tarmac, waiting for the growling approach of the C-17 aircraft, my legs were trembling. Tori stood with me, alongside the two other bereaved families, and it felt as if we were collectively holding our breath.

The military personnel made sure there were no surprises and the morning ran like clockwork. It was how they showed their respect to us – the families who had given everything. From the moment I had stepped off the plane at Heathrow, I had felt the arms of the military community wrapped around us all. We'd spent the previous night in a hotel near RAF Lyneham and now, as we stood waiting on the edge of the runway, I trembled at the thought that Mark was coming home.

It was only five days since they had knocked at my door, but time seemed to have no meaning any more. We'd been told exactly what to expect: the aircraft would fly past before circling and landing. Tori's face looked calm. She reminded me of her father. Her wide, thickly lashed eyes and arched brows were recognizably Mark's. Our eyes met. We both knew nothing needed to be said; this was a moment none of us could ever forget. Alongside us were other members of the family, plus Andy Moreland and Padre Simon.

Bang on time we all heard that unmistakeable rumble and the plane appeared through the clouds. It was flying low, and as it drew level it tipped its wings in acknowledgment. I could feel my heart thudding against my chest and took a deep breath, trying to remain calm. It seemed a powerful and fitting tribute to the families and the men they had lost.

There were three soldiers returning that day. The death toll had been very heavy in the previous few weeks. Mark was the longest-serving soldier to die in Afghanistan, with twenty-six years' service. He was also the 199th soldier to be killed on Operation Herrick, and there had been more since. I'd heard on the news that the number of lives lost in Afghanistan had now passed two hundred. That wasn't all of it either. There were hundreds more who had been critically injured and for whom life would never be the same. I couldn't help wishing that Mark had lost a leg but come back to us alive.

There was some communal shuffling as we went back inside the terminal to wait for the plane to land, and a little while later we filed outside to see the aircraft crouched on the runway. My breath came out in a shudder as I saw the open door to the hold at the back of the plane. An officer stood to salute as the first coffin emerged from inside. We'd been told in which order they would come off, so we all straightened up as Mark was walked slowly down the ramp. The steps of the soldiers were marked and in time but at the bottom of the ramp, as they levelled out, one of them made a fractional stumble. Afterwards, Andy said he wasn't surprised because Mark was a heavy bloke – probably the heaviest of the three.

The coffin was covered in a Union Jack, and as the six soldiers moved toward the robed Padre, I felt each step stamp home the painful reality of Mark's untimely homecoming. At that moment I wanted to run across and throw my arms around the coffin. As I thought my emotions were about to overpower me, the illicit trill of a mobile phone was a momentary distraction. We glanced around as people fumbled in pockets, and there was a titter of laughter, which somehow released the tension.

I was so glad the army had been able to get me to the base that day. It had been a close run thing a few days earlier, when Vince had discovered I didn't have a passport because it had run out, and I'd also lost my driving licence on our French holiday. Flying into the UK required valid photo ID. Miraculously, the regiment rushed through the paperwork and managed to get my new passport through in time. I could imagine Mark shaking his head; at least I hadn't been late to meet him this time.

Each of the coffins was taken to its own private chapel and a few minutes later Padre Simon took me through to be with Mark. It was the first time I had been alone with him since he had left a few weeks earlier. The coffin was bathed in an ethereal light as I entered the room, as if a spotlight had been thrown across it. I threw myself on top of it, wrapping my arms tightly around the sides. Tears were coursing down my cheeks and my whole body was shaking with deep sobs. At last I'd really begun to cry properly. I wanted to hold him, to tell him he shouldn't be coming home like this. There was a certain amount of relief having him there, but I wanted to get in the coffin with him to give him a hug.

I don't know how long I lay there, my hands gripping the sides of the coffin, and I was shaking. I felt someone peeling my fingers back one by one to help me let go. I couldn't bear to leave. I knew they would be taking him off to the John Radcliffe Hospital in Oxford. They had said it could be a while before he would be released by the coroner to be flown back home, and I didn't want to let him go again.

Staring at the flag-draped coffin, I said to myself, *This isn't about me; it's about Mark.* I took a deep breath and moved back as Mark's mum, Dianne, and Roger moved into the room.

A few minutes later, Andy Moreland stepped forward and patted the coffin gently before coming to stand beside me. He slid his arm around my shoulders. I was grateful for the touch. The coffin had felt so hard, so empty. The rational part of me knew it was, in a way. Simon had said a prayer earlier as I stood beside Mark, and he'd given him over to God's safekeeping. I knew the Mark we knew and loved was not here any more; he was with God, and I also knew we would be together again one day. I had to hold on to that hope, even in the midst of such terrible pain.

The journey to Wootton Bassett gave me time to recover as I stared out at the fields flashing past in a blur. I thought for a moment about all the other grieving wives and families. I'd gone to the Garrison church on Sunday. I knew it was the right thing to do. Everyone there knew the score, and many of them knew Mark. I was still moving about in a haze and hardly knew what I was saying. Another wife whose husband had been killed a few weeks before was in the congregation. She had a little baby who was six weeks old, and two other widows were attending the service that day as well. I remembered the Padre saying, "We gather here today to remember Mark Hale who was killed on Thursday…"

The Commanding Officer's wife Hilary, or Hils as we called her, had been there. We hugged and I was embraced by many others, including some of the Fijian wives whose husbands had been completely devastated by the news. There are a number of Fijians in the British armed forces, owing to Commonwealth links. There is a strong sense of community among them in many regiments. They called him "Brother Mark", and he had also been nicknamed "Chief" as they had looked up to him in so many ways: as a soldier, as a rugby player, and as a Christian they totally respected.

Tori and Alix didn't want to miss the procession through Wootton Bassett, so Nigel Moreland had taken them on ahead with his family. By the time I arrived, the crowds lining the street had begun to disperse and we headed for the pub where I knew most of Mark's old friends from the D&Ds would have gathered. As I approached I was enveloped in their welcome. There were so many people there who had come from all across the country to pay their respects. The pub was packed with people in every corner and seemed completely taken over by Mark's former army colleagues. There wasn't enough room inside, so dozens of people had spilled out onto the pavement, where they stood in small groups, clasping pints. So many had tears in their eyes; they were clearly shocked by his death.

"What are you drinking, Brenda?" One of them took my arm and steered me toward a table filled with beer glasses. Some of the lads were in suits, others in uniform, and some in their familiar D&D orange and green T-shirts. There were so many familiar faces everywhere I turned, and I wanted to make sure I spoke to as many of them as possible. They were in shock too, and in a way they were my family – my regimental family – so spending time with them was an important part of the day.

* * *

I leaned back against the car headrest. I was exhausted. Being buoyant and chatting at the pub had taken it out of me. More than two hundred had turned up to pay their respects to Mark. There were soldiers and ex-soldiers from all ranks, retired and serving. We'd reminisced and cried and laughed together. I had been so touched to see them, to feel their support, their love for me and the girls.

They had all said so many wonderful things about Mark, each one telling me a different story about his time as a young soldier, his wild days and street-fighting antics, his crazy fitness routines, that dry sense of humour, his unwavering loyalty and courage as a soldier. Many of them echoed the tribute paid by his Commanding Officer, Lieutenant Colonel Rob Thomson, who had described Mark as "undentable", a new word which he said summed up Mark as a soldier whom "nothing fazed" and who had a legendary ability "to absorb work, pressure, and other people's worries". I was quite overwhelmed by what I'd heard. I knew he was an incredible husband and father and that he was one of a kind, but I had never realized how many people he had had an impact on and how many lives he'd enriched during his twenty-six years in the army.

The car slowed down through a small village, and as we rounded a bend we could all see three long black vehicles heading toward us. We watched as they hummed past. Nothing was said, but we knew they were the same hearses returning empty from the mortuary in Oxford. It was a chilling reminder of what the day had been about.

Later that evening at Nigel Moreland's house, Nigel told Andy and me about the procession at Wootton Bassett and how his wife Jan had stopped and bought roses for the girls to put on the funeral car. "Alix couldn't reach," he said, "so I lifted her up so she could put it on the roof."

I nodded and sniffed. I would have wanted to be with them too, but I knew Mark was being taken away and I couldn't bear to shorten my time with him. "It was important for them to do that. Thanks for taking them."

It had been a hard day, and this was just the start. We all had the funeral to get through next. But before that, Mark would be coming home.

Tori and Alix's presence at Wootton Bassett had raised our profile with the media, and the next day their grieving faces were splashed across some of the tabloids. I was already concerned about the dangers of any of us being linked with the British army while we lived outside the wire. The previous week we'd decided to release photos of Mark in civilian clothes in an attempt to play down the military angle. The additional publicity was a concern. We were due to fly back to Belfast in a couple of days and had arranged to meet with Simon and Rachel Farmer at the airport, partly to talk about the funeral. Worried about the media trying to reach us, the airline switched our flight at the last minute and gave us a private room to meet in for half an hour before the flight. Leaving the girls enjoying some welcome hospitality in a special airline lounge under Andy's watchful eyes, I headed upstairs with Rachel and Simon.

It was a long time since I'd seen Rachel and we'd only recently reconnected on Facebook. As I started to explain what I knew about Mark's death and our last conversations, I could see Rachel's eyes filling with tears. "Don't you start," I said, "or you'll set me off again."

We laughed and we cried as we talked about aspects of the funeral and which hymns I'd already chosen. Simon had been our Padre for a few years while the regiment was based in Germany, and Rachel and I had been pregnant at the same time. Their youngest son Will was a few months younger than Tori.

I suppose I needed to talk about what had happened because it was my way of making sense of it all. "He didn't die straight away," I said. "He was so fit and strong. I know he must have been fighting to stay alive... he'd have probably been thinking,

'Brenda's gonna kill me if I don't make it.'" Their eyes widened and then we all saw the funny side of what I'd said.

I told Simon I definitely wanted two particular songs during the service. One of them was "Highland Cathedral". I'd heard it a few years earlier while Mark and I had been driving down to Devon. We'd been listening to the D&D regimental band CD and then "Highland Cathedral" had come on. I turned to Mark and said, "I'm going to have this at your funeral."

"Oh, that's cheerful," he'd said.

The other song I'd already chosen was "The Servant King" by Graham Kendrick. Mark and I had heard it at a little church in Cumbria where we'd been on holiday when Tori was a baby. When we'd heard the line "hands that flung stars into space", we'd both become really emotional as we thought, *This is the man who saved the world, and they stuck nails in His hands.*

Simon nodded. "That's a great song. Have you thought about who you want to speak and maybe do readings?"

We continued to discuss a few ideas and then I said, "I want you to preach. It's important that everyone hears the gospel. That's what Mark would have wanted. I want his friends to hear about him as a Christian soldier. You know Mark always used to say to the Padre, if they were leading a service for his soldiers, 'Make sure they hear the gospel. Don't lose this opportunity to preach to your soldiers.' He would say just the same for his funeral."

Simon told me about the last messages he and Mark had exchanged online, just a few days before he had been killed. He'd reminded Mark of a verse in the Bible, from Philippians 3:10: "I want to know Christ – yes, to know the power of his resurrection and participation in his sufferings, becoming like him in his death." I fought back my tears as he said Mark had been God's hands and feet as he'd walked the villages and fields of Helmand

Province. It was true. I knew it was true. Some moments I could see all that and I knew my life was in God's hands. Mark and I had both believed that. It was just so hard to walk this path on my own, without Mark by my side. All I had now was God to lean on, and I suppose that's what I had to learn to do.

"In Captain Mark Hale,
a very great man has fallen –
in fact, many of us know that
a great warrior has fallen."

The Revd (Major) Simon Farmer

CHAPTER 22

1 September 2009

... a time to honour

Each corner of the flag was held and folded deliberately as the soldiers turned it into a neat, padded triangle. Mark's belt, his hat, and his medals were laid on top, before they were handed to the uniformed officer at the side of the grave. Moments later, as the coffin was lowered into the ground, the Padre's words hung in the air like the drizzle that was forming a fine mist on all our dark coats and jackets.

"I am the resurrection and the life: he that believeth in me, though he were dead, yet shall he live."

Yet shall he live. All around me our friends and family stared into that grave and, like me, they must have wished for another scene. None of us wanted to say goodbye to Mark like this.

"Earth to earth, ashes to ashes, dust to dust..."

Something heavy slid down inside me as I heard the soil splatter on the wood below. It felt as if a part of me was being buried there in the ground with him. As I looked around, I saw Andy Moreland's legs bending toward the grave, and Dianne reached out her arm to steady him. It was a picture of how I felt. *How can we stand without you, Mark?*

* * *

The previous night he had been at home with us for the last time. When I'd heard he was finally due to be brought back by the undertakers, I was suddenly nervous and panicked. I turned to Vince. "What do I do? I don't know what to do."

He patted my hand and said, "Your man's coming home. What do you normally do when he's coming home?"

I hesitated, "I... I get dressed up... I get my nails done and..."

"Go on, then. Go and get changed, put on his favourite clothes, and do your make-up."

My teeth were chattering again and I was shaking even in the shower, but I found the black silk shirt that Mark loved. I had worn it when I had met him coming back for R&R just four weeks earlier. Sliding my arms into the sleeves, I began shakily fastening up the buttons. I did my make-up, adding a touch of lippy, and sprayed a puff of perfume. I was ready.

* * *

I'd asked Andy and Simon to stay in the house that night, and when the undertakers closed the door behind them, I went into the front room on my own. The curtains were closed and the light was soft. The lid of the coffin had been taken off and I moved to stand beside it. He was dressed in his desert combats and it was almost as if he was just sleeping. Part of me was so happy to have him home; it's what I'd been waiting for. He was where he should be.

I stroked his face and talked to him. There were things I needed to say. Then I went out, took the girls by the hand, and we went in to be with him. Alix had drawn a picture of a rainbow with us all standing under it. She laid it in the coffin with her daddy, along with a friendship bracelet she had made to send out to him. Tori added in a laminated photograph of her with Mark, taken when she was about six on our holiday in Australia. She had been using it as a bookmark and had carried it with her everywhere since he had died.

I wanted to sleep in the room with him that night; I couldn't bear for him to be alone. Instead we all sat on the floor beside Mark with Simon and Andy, while Simon led a communion service. The words seemed to have special meaning at that moment: "We break this bread... to share in the body of Christ." Simon's voice was hushed but steady.

Then we said together, "Though we are many, we are one body, because we all share in one bread."

As I sipped the wine and ate the bread, the final words about Jesus opening the gate of glory stayed with me. It was comforting to know that Mark was with God now. We had both believed in that promise of eternal life, and it seemed so right to be sharing communion with Mark in the room, all together as a family.

After the girls had gone to bed, Andy showed me the stable belt he had borrowed from Mark years earlier when they had been serving in Berlin. It was made from webbing in the D&D colours of green and orange, with leather buckles. I remembered Mark wearing one the same.

"When you rang and told me, something made me think about it and I went to find it," he said. He showed me how it still had Mark's name inside. "I borrowed it and never gave it back. It was his spare," he explained. "I'm going to cut it in half and put one half in with Mark. The other half will be buried with me."

I knew it meant a lot to Andy, because he'd lost a great friend, an irreplaceable friend.

* * *

The next morning I stared across at the packet of Valium that my sister Alison had run out to fetch for me. She thought I would need it to get through the day. I shook my head as I dressed. *I'm meant to feel this.* I didn't take the tablets because I wanted to remember the day. I wanted to be there for Mark, and for everyone else who was grieving too.

The girls came into the bedroom. They both looked beautiful dressed in black, Tori's long wavy hair was shining and Alix had fixed on her velvet headband. As I adjusted my hat in the mirror, I wished Mark could see how lovely they looked. Whatever happened today, his girls would do him proud. I could hear his voice in my head singing to us, "Here come the girls!"

Gillian put her head around the door. "Have you eaten anything, Brenda?"

I shook my head. "I've had coffee; I'll be fine."

"The cars have arrived," she said.

I trembled at the thought of Mark being taken away, but by the time I was downstairs they had already moved the coffin into the car. Around the cul-de-sac people were at their doors, standing watching as we got into the cars, and the journey began. I clasped the girls' hands in mine. *Today we will face it together. Today we're a unit again.*

We stood and watched as the soldiers carried him up the steps into the church. The coffin was wrapped in the Union Jack. The dark grey stone of the building rose up in front of us, its huge cathedral-like doors yawning open. It wasn't our church, but it was the only place that would hold the numbers that were due to attend. It was also somewhere that the army felt would be secure for such a high-profile military funeral.

Even with the family at our side, I had a foretaste of the isolation that lay ahead. It seeped through me like a cold fluid running through my veins. As we stood at the foot of the steps,

I slid my arms around both girls while we heard the majestic sounds of the piper playing "Highland Cathedral" echoing round the building. Inside, the faces of so many friends and strangers turned to welcome us, and my heart swelled with pride for the man they had come to acknowledge. This was for the soldier I had married, who had laid down his life on the battlefield.

The words of the Padre, reading from Romans, echoed my own thoughts. "I am convinced that neither death nor life, neither angels nor demons, neither the present nor the future, nor any powers, neither height nor depth, nor anything else in all creation, will be able to separate us from the love of God that is in Christ Jesus our Lord."

Hymns, songs, readings, and eulogies left me close to tears all through the service, but each tribute I heard made me more and more proud of Mark. He'd meant everything to us, but he'd also had such an impact on others. Padre Simon described him in the address as a "Christian warrior", and that is exactly what he was. There were so many moments to treasure from the service, most especially the farewell song by the Fijian wives, which they sang as Mark left the church. Vince had told me that their husbands had sung the same song at Camp Bastion as Mark was being put in the plane to come home. They had asked if they could stand in for their husbands today. It was a beautiful sound and so fitting for the rugby-playing soldier they counted as one of their own.

The number of people at the service was quite overwhelming. Some two hundred former and serving Devonshire and Dorset Regiment soldiers had flown in from Exeter on a specially commissioned Hercules. As they were due to fly back shortly after the service, I made sure I met with as many of them as possible in a room near the church. Their presence was humbling, and the collective support and care for us as a family was such a comfort.

It was as if God had organized all these people to wrap us up with love and care. They were standing in the huge gap that had opened up in our family.

When I got into the car with trembling legs to go to the burial, I knew we would get through the day, and then the next day. Somehow we would have to do it one day at a time.

* * *

Suddenly the silence was shattered as a volley of gunshots rang out above our heads. There was a finality about the sound of that gunfire as it echoed across the graves. I closed my eyes, picturing Mark standing to attention in his uniform, his rifle against his shoulder, his gloved hand clenched at his side. Brigadier Richard Toomey, a former CO of Mark's and his platoon commander years before, stepped toward me, holding the stack of the flag and the medals. I straightened up and we looked at each other as he placed the precious bundle in my arms. "Brenda, this is not the time and place. We shouldn't be meeting like this," he whispered.

I couldn't speak. But many other happy times when we had all been together – regimental parties, dinners, and barbecues, even down on the beach with the sand buggy – flashed into my mind. Receiving Mark's medals from Richard felt absolutely right. I wouldn't have wanted it to be anyone else.

*"A legend – a giant of a man in every
sense of the word.
Honourable, intelligent, utterly
professional, and loyal."*

**Lieutenant Colonel (now Major General)
Rupert Jones**

CHAPTER 23

October 2009

... a time to pray

I don't know how long I had been lying there; it could have been minutes or even hours. I'd stopped screaming and now my sobs had subsided into small hiccups and sniffs. The official army letter lay next to me on the kitchen floor. Something had snapped inside me when I'd read it, and the weeks of silent grieving, trying to be strong, and being so British about everything had finally made me crack.

When I'd read the words that Mark had been discharged from the army, I didn't know what to do with it. *How could they discharge him when he was already dead?* I didn't know what to do with the letter; I didn't even know what it really meant. All the money worries over mortgage payments, the mess over Mark's missing will, the visits to the bank, the phone calls, and trying to fight the system had taken its toll.

Captain Vince Mears had been sent back to serve in Afghanistan three weeks after the funeral and I'd been handed over to a different visiting officer. After a week that VO had also gone and the army gave me a phone number to call in the UK if I needed anything. It seemed that with the number of deaths happening, there simply weren't enough visiting officers to go round. The regiment were still on deployment and more soldiers were being killed. I felt so alone, as if I had no one to talk to, no one to help me. Mark usually handled all the army admin. If he had been around I would have just given the letter to him and he would have sorted it out at work. I closed my eyes, running back over the past few weeks in my head.

The money worries had started almost straight away. Just after Mark had died, I went to see Lt Col Rob Thomson, Mark's CO, who was back on leave. He sat down with me in their sitting room and asked if there was anything he could do to help.

"I have no money to pay Alix's school fees," I said.

Alix had just started prep school in the same school as Tori, but the army didn't give any help with prep school fees.

"Leave it with me," Rob said. He was as good as his word and within a few days I heard that the Army Benevolent Fund and the Rifles Association would cover her fees for the next three years. That was one less thing to worry about and I felt so grateful, but I knew they couldn't solve everything.

Mark's wages were stopped the day he died. They told me he had died at 9.17 a.m., so he effectively hadn't turned up for work that day, which meant he wasn't entitled to a full day's pay. The army procedure felt brutal at times. I knew Mark had made a will, as had all his other D&D mates when they had deployed to Iraq. We were still living at the same house, so the details remained unchanged. I was told the regiment had been unable to find the will. I couldn't understand it because I knew Mark had made one. It meant everything would now have to go through probate, the legal process to prove who was entitled to the funds, before it could be released to the girls and me. They said it could take up to eighteen months. In the meantime we needed to eat, pay the bills, and put diesel in the car. I remember crying silently into my pillow that night, not wanting the girls to hear me. I needed to provide for them. I had no Mark now to be strong and look after us. It was just me, and I didn't know how we were going to manage.

In the week before Mark's death the little house we'd been renting out in Bangor had finally been sold and the money transferred into our account. Not wanting to lose out on interest, I'd sunk it into a long-term saver account. I thought if I could get the bank to release it, I would be able to manage until the other funds came through. After all, I'd only just put it there a week before. When I went into the bank they told me it wasn't possible to get at the funds, even in exceptional circumstances, and they offered to give me a loan instead. I didn't want to be in debt or take out a loan.

Feeling as if I kept walking down blind alleys, when I got home I rang Nigel Moreland. Nigel, who had started out in the Marines, was now an army lawyer. We talked about what was happening and he said he'd make some phone calls, telling me not to worry. It wasn't easy not to feel panicky. My salary as a teaching assistant had only been holiday money and went nowhere near covering the cost of the mortgage, let alone everything else we needed. *What if the girls need new kit at school? What about Christmas?* Not only had they lost their daddy, it also felt as if we'd lost everything. If we didn't pay the mortgage, we could lose our home.

Nigel rang me back sometime later and said he had asked for a "mortgage holiday" for us, and hopefully that would give me a breather. I was thankful, but still uncertain about how long that would last.

Pushing myself up off the floor, I washed my face at the sink and dabbed it dry with a towel. I snatched up the letter and added it to the pile of papers I would have to tackle at some point.

Later that evening, just after Alix had gone to bed, I was going through my emails trying to delete unwanted ones. I kept coming across messages from Mark. I clicked on one that had been sent not long after he had deployed: "Hope everything OK. We're going through our induction. Apparently this place is luxury compared to where we're heading..."

Then I clicked on another one further down. He was telling me about the rowing challenge he'd organized. They were rowing the distance from Sangin to Pegasus Bridge to tie in with the anniversary of the D-Day landings and help raise money for wounded soldiers. He was encouraging everyone else to do their part and row a minimum of 10,000 metres a day. To up the stakes, in one inhuman session Mark had rowed 42,000 metres, watching three films to stop the boredom.

A bit later, he had written:

> *Hiya honey,*
> *Well, the start of another week. I know that you shouldn't wish your life away, but it is very difficult not to when you are so desperate to get home...*
> *Not sure what you're doing. Wish I was there with you.*
> *Love you so much xxxx*

Reading his emails was a bit like hearing his voice. Inside, my heart was crumbling. *I wish we could turn the clock back, my darling...*

The phone started ringing and I was jolted back to reality.

"Good evening," said a man's voice with a distinctive Northern Irish accent that was vaguely familiar. "Could I speak with Brenda Hale, please?"

"Speaking," I said, racking my brains to think who it might be.

"It's Jeffrey Donaldson here. I wondered if I could call round to see you on my way home tonight?"

It seemed rude to say no: this was my local MP. He said he would be driving straight from the airport and would be here in about half an hour. I quickly tidied up the kitchen and pinched some colour into my pale cheeks. The last time I had spoken to him had been before Mark was killed.

It was just after Mark had left for Afghanistan that I had decided to start doing something for myself. I'd been an army wife for twenty-two years, and I'd been the one keeping the home fires burning. Like so many military wives, I'd put my own interests to one side because husband, regiment, and children came first. That spring, with Alix turning eight, I decided to see how I could become more actively involved in the local Democratic Unionist Party. I wanted to start putting the degree I'd taken to good use.

Politics had been a long-running passion of mine, so I rang the MP's constituency office, offering to volunteer, and Jeffrey Donaldson got back to me quite quickly. He asked for a few personal details and why I wanted to volunteer. The European elections were coming up and he said it would be good if I could help canvass. Then he asked a bit more about my background and I told him about Mark, who had just deployed to Afghanistan. He said, "I pray for a safe return."

I laughed and said, "So do I."

Everything in my life was now fixed as events before or after Mark's death. That previous phone conversation could have been yesterday, yet it seemed a world away now. I brought Jeffrey through to the kitchen and we sat down at the table with mugs of tea. I didn't have to explain everything that had happened because there had been a lot in the media about Mark, especially on local TV and in the newspapers. After I'd given an interview to the *Sunday Times* there had been TV crews outside the house and frequent media calls in the past few weeks, which first Vince and then others had shielded me from.

Jeffrey leaned forward across the table and told me how sorry he was to hear about Mark's death. "Is there anything I can do to help, Brenda? Please do tell me."

I hesitated for a moment. It was after ten o'clock and the evenings were always the hardest. I could sense the genuine care in his voice and felt my eyes filling with tears. I couldn't stop myself crying, but when I calmed my voice I said, "Do you really mean that? Are you really here to offer help?"

When he said he was I said, "I have no money. They can't find his will and there is no money going into my bank account. Surely there has to be more that can be done?"

He looked completely shocked. I knew Jeffrey had served in the Ulster Defence Regiment and his brother had been in the Royal Tank Regiment, so he had a reasonable knowledge of how the military worked. I explained how helpless I felt and how I had now lost my visiting officer. Each time I had to contact a VO in England, I had to go through a system on the phone of giving Mark's name, army number, rank, and the date of his death. There were days when running through those details was too painful, and I was simply trying to get through each hour without breaking down.

Jeffrey turned to me and said, "No wife who has lost her husband in service to her country should have to go through this."

He seemed genuinely upset by what he'd heard, and as he left he said, "Leave this with me, Brenda; I'll see what I can do."

* * *

I walked a lonely path in the weeks that followed. Trying to hold myself together for the girls, I hid my fears about the finances and forced myself to think a day at a time. My church minister Bobby Liddle was a great support, along with other people from the church and my family and friends. A few days after Jeffrey's visit I had intended to go through some paperwork, but ended up thumbing through an envelope full of old holiday photos from France. The phone rang again and a strange voice asked for me.

"Yes, speaking," I said tentatively. I was worried it could be someone from the media again. They could be very persistent.

"It's Margaret Mervis here, Paul's mother."

I was astounded and pleased to hear from her. She was the mother of Lt Paul Mervis, who had been killed in Afghanistan a few weeks before Mark. Someone had told her about the article in *The Times* and she was ringing to thank me for mentioning Paul in the interview. Paul had been a great soldier and his death had rocked everyone, including Mark. As we talked, Margaret said, "Do you have everything you need, Brenda?"

I hesitated, and then said, "I'm worried because I haven't paid the mortgage this month."

She seemed surprised and said I should be getting a similar amount to Mark's wages coming into my bank account each month.

"All I have had is the state widow's pension of £400 a month, and it doesn't cover the mortgage," I explained.

Margaret told me she was a barrister and offered to make some enquiries on my behalf. She worked wonders, and within days she'd discovered that the lump sum payment I was due from the army on Mark's death had been bouncing back because the bank details were incorrect. Without a VO on hand to help sort it out and speak with the army accounts office, I'd been helpless. But with Margaret working magic behind the scenes, it was eventually sent through to the right account.

* * *

Toward the end of October Nigel and Jan Moreland came to stay. I was hoping they would help me sort out some of the finance issues and how to deal with probate.

I dropped the heavy tin box of files down on the table. "This has all our finances in it. Mark had it all in order," I said, looking across at Nigel, who began to thumb through the neatly divided sections from car insurance to bank information.

An image of Mark sitting at the kitchen table with the box beside him in March flashed into my head. He had been doing the tax returns and getting all the accounts in order before he left. He turned around to where I was packing dishes into the dishwasher and said, "See this, Brenda, when it comes to next January, you have to make sure the accountant gets all the tax returns."

I stared at him. *He'll be here in January; why is he saying that?* My voice sounded cross. "I'm not doing it; that's your job."

More quietly he said, "I'm just reminding you, that's all."

Each conversation I recalled from before he left was tainted with uncertainty. I'd blanked it out at the time, but now it all seemed to fit together, like the missing pieces of a jigsaw.

Nigel looked up from sorting through the documents. "It all looks incredibly organized," he said.

It certainly was. Mark had been meticulous about keeping it all in order. He'd been like that about his degree work and the Master's, getting down to work straight away. He was very focused. I was the opposite. It used to take me ages to knuckle down to an essay. The house would be spotless by the time I started writing or reading because I'd find a million things to do and clean before I could settle.

Nigel had made an appointment for us to meet with a solicitor he worked with in Belfast so that I could begin the process of going through probate. When we walked into the office the solicitor reached out to shake my hand and smiled. "It's a privilege to meet you," he said. As we all sat down around his desk he told us he'd been inspired by reading about Mark in the *Presbyterian*

Herald. I remembered that the Presbyterian moderator, John Stafford Carson, had said he would like to write something about Mark's faith as a soldier, after visiting me a few weeks ago.

"Which church do you go to?" I asked, amazed that out of all the solicitors Nigel could have chosen, he had found one who was a Christian. As we talked about what had happened and the issues with the will, he explained about the process. He seemed so thoughtful, and then when I asked about the fee, he shook his head.

"I won't be charging for this; it's the least I can do."

As I left I was amazed. Somehow God had been putting people in the right place at the right time. As I fell and thought I was about to crash, Christians had been there to catch me, to help me each step of the way. I may have felt alone, but I wasn't really. My heavenly Father was walking right next to me and holding my hand.

"His calm appearance contrasted with a fierce determination to support all he knew; whether it be his family, fellow Riflemen, or even teammates on a rugby pitch."

Captain (now Major) Rupert Streatfeild

CHAPTER 24

November 2009

... a time to remember

I turned the tickets over in my hands. We'd booked our flights to Australia back in February before Mark had left. It was to be a long overdue visit to see Andy and Kathy Moreland. The last time we'd been there was in 1999 when Tori had just started school, and Alix hadn't even been born. I couldn't imagine being there without Mark, but as no refund was possible, it seemed a waste not to use the flights. The travel company weren't able to transfer Mark's ticket into Gillian's name, so she had bought a new ticket to come with us and we were all due to leave in a few days. I stared down at the open suitcases. I needed to muster up the enthusiasm to start packing. It wasn't that I didn't want to see Andy and Kathy and their son Ben, but I couldn't deny it was going to be hard. I knew we would all be haunted by memories of the last visit, aware of the empty seat at the table.

It was going to be hot, and I pulled open the cupboard doors, wondering if I even had a bikini that was still decent. I noticed the brightly coloured shopping bag at the bottom of the cupboard and pulled it out. Inside was the pair of new board shorts I had bought for Mark a couple of months earlier. He'd had a washboard stomach and, once he'd got a tan, I knew he would have looked amazing in them. I pushed them back into the bag and took a deep breath. *I'm just packing for me and the girls this time*, I said to myself. But even as I pulled open drawers and began to pile clothes onto the bed, I could feel tears sliding down my cheeks. *Who are you trying to fool, Brenda?*

That trip in 1999 had been an amazing holiday. We'd gone on a boat ride to Fraser Island. I looked across at the corner of the room where the infamous didgeridoo was leaning against the wall. I remembered trying to talk to Kathy above the deafening noise because Mark and Andy had bought one each and would have competitions over who could play the loudest and the longest. They would sit on the settee and keep blowing them, and we'd be shouting at them to stop.

We'd been excited when we'd booked the flights and we'd hoped it would be the light at the end of the tunnel that would help us get through that dark tour. I had never imagined that we would be going without him.

I slid down onto the floor beside the bed and put my head in my hands. This was Mark's side of the bed. The day after we'd got the news, Tori had dragged her mattress into the room and arranged it on the floor next to his side of the bed. Ever since, both the girls had slept in my room each night: Alix in the bed where Mark had slept and Tori on the mattress beside us.

"Oh Mark, I can't do this," I said through shuddering breaths.

Last week I'd been at the grave; it was where I felt closest to him. Mark had chosen Legacurry as the church for us to attend, and somehow that was where I felt I could talk to him. The freshly dug earth had now become a low grass mound. I'd run my hands along the smooth oak of the cross that Nigel Moreland had made. He'd even fixed a brass plaque with the inscription "Captain Mark Hale". It would be some months before we would be able to put up the stone.

I'd crouched down beside the cross. I was grateful to have the marker. It stood head and shoulders above all the other graves, which seemed appropriate because Mark was usually head and shoulders above most people. It had been raining so the grass was soaked. Little droplets of rain slid off the smooth wood of the cross and gathered like tears glistening on the metal of the plaque.

I hadn't been planning to be there that afternoon. Vince Mears had phoned me on his way home from Afghanistan. "Brenda," he'd said, "the Fijians are landing in Aldergrove this afternoon, and before they go on to Ballykilner they've asked if they can go to visit Mark. Is that OK? They would like you to be there."

I said I'd meet them. I was moved that they were coming straight to Mark's graveside from Afghanistan, even before going home to see their wives and families. As the bus drew up, they all poured down the steps, and I could see they were crying. These were great, tough, rugby-playing guys, and they were sobbing. One by one they sat down on the wet grass, forming a circle around the grave, and they started to sing. It was the same Fijian farewell song their wives had sung at the funeral. The sound of their harmonious voices rose up into the damp air and I felt myself trembling at its beauty. Then they prayed and sang again. The whole thing went on for about an hour. It was as if they were mourning one of their own family, but I suppose in a way they were – he was their "brother Mark".

After they had left, I looked around the graveyard, taking in the rows of headstones marking other loved ones who were also dearly missed. Mark's was the first war grave in this small country churchyard.

* * *

I'd made Mark take me to the war graves years ago when I'd visited him in Berlin while we were engaged. It had been a lovely hot summer in Germany and we'd enjoyed time exploring the parks, seeing the sights in the day, and partying hard in the nightclubs in the evenings. Even though he wasn't off the whole time, I stayed with some of his friends and would go to the swimming pool on the base, and he would get out to see me in the evenings. Part of his duties included guarding Rudolf Hess in Spandau Prison, which seemed incredible to me. I'd only heard that name in history lessons. During the holiday I told him I wanted to visit the war graves.

"No, I'm not taking you, Brenda, you'll only cry," he'd said.

"But I really want to go and see the war graves, Mark."

In the end, he'd given in and taken me to the Commonwealth War Cemetery in Berlin. I could still picture the white walls and walking through the black wrought-iron gates to be faced with hundreds of white headstones. I remembered thinking, *These are all just boys who died far away from home*. I couldn't help it and I started to sob, tears running down my face. Mark took my hand and said, "Come on, we're leaving."

But I turned toward the stand where the visitors' book sat open. "No, I want to write in the book first," I said. Wiping my eyes, I simply wrote, "Thank you."

* * *

The day we were due to leave for Australia was also the regiment's homecoming medals parade at Abercorn Barracks. I wanted to see everyone, but knew I couldn't cope with seeing them all march on and receive their medals when Mark and so many others were missing. But we'd been invited to the CO's house so that we could attend the lunch and the church service.

Rob and Hilary Thomson welcomed us as warmly as ever. The church service to mark the end of the tour was held in the main gym because it was the only place large enough to hold the whole battalion. After the service I managed to speak to some of the Fijian families and others I hadn't seen since Mark had been killed.

There was the usual curry lunch at the Officers' Mess before the parade. I'd been to a fair few homecoming parties, but this was like nothing I'd ever attended before. The setting was the same and the army chicken curry tasted just the same, but everything else had changed. The huge silver trays were set out at one end with heated plates, and people were heaping on the various curry options, with poppadoms balanced on the side. Several officers were propping up the bar at one end, while children were being seated at tables to avoid food being spread around the deep patterned carpet.

As I perched at the edge of a table with the girls, I looked around and felt the deep sadness running through the room. The atmosphere was thick with grief. It felt as if the whole room had been shell-shocked. I could feel the two missing officers, Paul and Mark, as if they were moving about among the battalion like living ghosts. There were guys in wheelchairs with no legs and people with missing arms. This was the same bunch of men and women who had been fit and healthy a few months earlier, and who had partied hard before leaving for the operation. The mood today was deeply reflective. There was no laughter, no raucous drinking. At most, there was a low mumble of conversation.

After lunch Tori and Alix went with the Thomsons to the parade and I stayed at their house to look after the youngest addition to the family, Rory, who was five months old. When they had left, I slipped on my jacket. Pushing Rory in his huge Silver Cross pram, I strode out along the empty roads of the base beneath a steely grey sky. It was almost three months since Mark had died. That day was another milestone I had been dreading – seeing the regiment return and the families reunited with their loved ones. Mark not being among them felt like a physical stab in my chest each time I thought of him. It wasn't that I hadn't felt supported and cared for by the regiment; they still wanted me to be a part of everything and I was invited to all the events. But kindness couldn't heal my wounds or salve the pain I felt.

I heard the distant shout of the drill sergeant, carried by the breeze, calling the parade to a halt. I increased my pace along the tarmac road and felt the wind massaging my face and whipping my hair out to the sides. I remembered how Mark took his drill practice so seriously. Just before we moved to London where he was about to be a colour sergeant, he was seriously challenged by how to march with a stick. Marching had been bad enough, but twisting and moving the stick required real coordination. I could picture him now, marching up and down from the kitchen through to the dining room, his face set straight ahead.

"Let me have a feel of the stick," I said as he paused, frustrated that he still couldn't get it right.

I twiddled it effortlessly in one hand. He stared at me. "How did you do that?"

I giggled and threw it back to him. He caught it and started trying to turn it himself.

The memory made me smile. Coordination was not his strong point, but Mark had persevered until he was perfect at it. He'd never give up.

The sky seemed to be darkening. As I turned a corner in the road, a perfect rainbow suddenly appeared, arching across the sky. I immediately thought of Mark and the rainbow Alix had drawn and how we'd seen the rainbow after my mummy had died. I prayed then and silently thanked God for the years I had enjoyed with Mark. I was grateful for the time we'd been given.

A little while later we hugged our friends goodbye and headed out to the car that would take us to the airport. I knew the pain and damage that had cut through our family on 13 August had rippled out to others. There were so many hurting people in the building behind us, and beyond that in other parts of the country where military families had lost sons and daughters, husbands and wives, fathers and mothers. We were not alone.

CHAPTER 25

April 2010

... a time to speak up

The towering face of Big Ben was the first thing I saw as we emerged from the tube station. I was on my way to Whitehall with my MP Jeffrey Donaldson for a meeting with the Minister of Defence. Across the road the iconic architecture of the Houses of Parliament fanned out before me, just beyond the reach of the milling crowds on the pavements. It seemed like a fortress, with high wrought-iron railings encircling the building and police positioned strategically beside each opening. My father's voice echoed in my head: "Let's see if it's different with a woman in charge."

I was nine years old when Margaret Thatcher was elected. My dad had said to me, "This is history – the first female prime minister in the western world." I became hooked into politics from that point on. My treat, when I was younger, was to stay up and watch the nine o'clock news. *In my generation everyone has an opinion, and it's always the right one, no matter who voices it!* My dad was quite political. He worked in the shipyards most of his life.

He was a Labour voter and fiercely loyal to the trade union movement. We used to have big discussions at home. I enjoyed the cut and thrust, and he would often say, "No, Brenda, you're wrong."

My mum told me he missed me when I moved away, partly because I was the only one who would argue with him about politics. He loved that I thought things through for myself and that I had independence of mind, because the last thing he wanted was a clone of himself. My father believed that if you had a conviction about something and you had good reasons for that, then your position should be respected. He taught me an enormous amount about having respect for those who hold a different viewpoint. My dad hated Maggie Thatcher for closing down the mines, because lots of my cousins were miners in Yorkshire. In fact, many of the family were high up in the miners' union during the strikes in the 1980s. I took a much more right-wing position and he couldn't convince me otherwise. I saw myself as a Tory with a conscience.

I was sad that my father's Alzheimer's disease had taken hold so rapidly. He didn't always know who I was now and kept asking when Mum was coming back. On other days we would talk about the girls and what they were doing at school. I was upset that his once sharp mind was fading fast. I hadn't been able to talk to him about Mark; it was too painful, because I knew the next day he would have forgotten. It was a massive blow that I couldn't share my grief with him, and somehow it deepened my sense of isolation.

* * *

It felt strange to be walking down Whitehall with Jeffrey Donaldson. We'd caught the flight from Belfast together and, although I felt supported by him, I was very pleased to see

Roger Cleave's familiar frame hovering outside the blank-looking windows of the government building. Roger, who worked nearby, was Mark's former company commander and a great friend. He had agreed to come with me for moral support. Part of me didn't know what on earth I was doing coming here to lobby a cabinet member. It wasn't even a year since Mark had been killed. *Who am I to start campaigning for the military and their families? But if I don't speak out, who will?*

When I'd spoken to Jeffrey about Mark's death a few weeks after the funeral and explained what was happening to us, he had said he wanted to help. He was true to his word. A few months later, he had asked me if I would be prepared to speak directly with the Defence Secretary, Bob Ainsworth, if he could arrange a meeting.

Inside the vast lobby a security guard checked our ID and traced his finger down a list for our names. I was nervous. I brushed my hands down my jacket and stared down at the top of my black patent shoes peeping out beneath my grey trousers. Roger caught my eye and winked as the guard waved us through.

The more I'd thought about the injustice of what had happened to us with the financial struggles and confusion I'd experienced, and the more I heard of similar stories from other bereaved wives and families, I knew I couldn't stay silent. The death toll in Afghanistan was continuing to rise and yet the government didn't seem to be making sure the families of those who had paid the ultimate price were being cared for properly. After that first visit, Jeffrey had raised questions in the House of Commons about the care for bereaved families. He had also been a regular visitor to our house every few weeks, calling in to check on how we were.

Jeffrey Donaldson is from the south of County Down and was brought up in a rural Presbyterian family. His first taste of the Troubles was when his cousin, who was an RUC constable, was murdered. He was the first policeman to be blown up by the IRA during the Troubles. Some years later, while Mark was serving in Northern Ireland with the army, one of Jeffrey's uncles was killed in a mortar attack on Newry police station. Jeffrey had launched himself into the thick of politics from an early age, and I admired what he'd achieved. He was also a practising Christian and attended his local Presbyterian church. He now operated at the highest levels in both Stormont and Westminster.

As we followed him down the bare corridors of power, the building reminded me of a slightly upmarket school, and our shoes squeaked as we paced down the passageways lined with closed doors. Then we moved through some more modernized sections of the building which had open-plan offices, and we were shown into a side room with glass doors and windows off the main workstations. Bob Ainsworth was sitting at a table, with three or four colleagues either side of him in crisp shirts. His neatly cropped hair was greying and his moustache and wire-rimmed glasses were reminiscent of an elder statesman. We shook hands and took our seats, then Jeffrey briefly explained some background, before the Minister turned to look at me.

His question was almost a challenge: "What's wrong?"

I thought, *Given that he's a Minister, it's not good that he doesn't know what's going on.*

I took a deep breath and said, "Let me give you a list of what went wrong for us after Mark was killed." I didn't hold back as I told him about the numerous VOs, no money, and one part of the army not speaking to the other part of the army. As I relayed my experiences over the past few months, I was crying as I spoke. I felt Roger rub my back, trying to help me regain my composure as I finally said, "In the meantime, the people falling through the net are young children, bereaved wives, and bereaved parents."

I could see he was moved. I suppose this was the first time he was seeing raw grief as a result of our war and mass destruction in Afghanistan. This was where policy met the person. He was visibly emotional as he apologized, and then he said, "We have no money."

I said, "Army families don't want money. They only want what they're entitled to: pensions, continuation of school fees, and recognition for a life lost in service." Once I'd started to speak, the words seemed to flow. "We just want to be looked after – we're not after dovecotes and moats. Don't tell me you have no money: you have three Labour MPs who have been caught with their hands in the till and you've allowed legal aid for them at millions of pounds! But you've no money for soldiers. I believe very strongly that the Westminster government has a moral obligation to look after our soldiers and their families when they come back damaged from war or if they come back in a box."

Roger said afterwards that I was a force of nature. Someone had told me Mark had written a note to the VO on his next of kin form which had said, "Beware fiery Irish woman." He was right, and that day I felt ready to go into battle on behalf of all those grieving families who needed support from the government that had sent their loved ones into danger.

The outcome was that the Defence Secretary promised a review into the military covenant and specifically how it dealt with bereaved families. It was a start.

"As a father he was deeply proud of his daughters; as a soldier he was deeply paternal toward his men. His strong and caring nature came from his close faith and relationship with God."

Captain (now Major) Rupert Streatfeild

CHAPTER 26

May 2010

... a time to uproot

Those gorgeous green eyes stared out from the photograph and I ran my finger down the image, trailing across the side of his face and lips. I felt a lone tear slide down my cheek. My recent meeting in Westminster seemed a million miles from this reality. This was real life – finding photographs of my dead husband and thinking about leaving a house with memories of him in every room. And it was hard, so much harder than before. We would usually have a bit of a clear-out before a move, and there would inevitably be fights over what we would keep and what was going to get chucked or given away.

Moving from Warminster had involved a particularly painful clear-out. Mark had decided it was time to get rid of all Tori's baby things, which I'd been holding on to just in case we had another child. We were also anxious about all the letters from each other that we had both kept. There were hundreds, and some of them were very explicit, because we'd corresponded for more than two years before we were married and throughout numerous periods of separation while Mark was away. Tori was seven and we both felt worried about her finding them and reading them. We didn't want to upset or shock her, so we decided to get rid of them. One evening after she'd gone to bed, Mark bought a couple of bottles of wine and we started a bonfire in the back garden. Eager flames licked up the sides of the old pallets and boxes that Mark had used to start the fire. We sat on two garden chairs with the boxes of letters between us. As I took a sip of wine from a glass, Mark fished out one of the letters and began to read it aloud. We laughed and giggled together and then we took it in turns to throw them into the fire, watching it guzzle up the paper like a ferocious tiger.

We only kept the first ten letters and all the rest were burned – more than one thousand letters. I remembered how the long blue envelopes used to fall on the mat by the door at home and everyone would tease me that the postman only came for me. I wished I had those letters now. *I wish we hadn't done that.* Now, with Tori almost seventeen, I knew it would have been OK for her to see them when she was an adult. At least then she would have known what a close emotional relationship we had, because she couldn't see that any more. Neither Tori nor Alix would catch us sneaking a kiss in the kitchen before tea or holding hands as we walked along a beach. Those letters would have given them an insight into what a close marriage looked like and what being in love felt like. I slid the photograph back into the packet with the others and dropped it into the box. *I can't do this*, I thought. *There's no way I can pack up our things.* In the end I didn't have to.

* * *

I'd decided to move house. I'm not sure exactly when I first realized it would be a good idea. We'd lived in Dromara for six years and the house held many happy memories, but often those memories were painful too. Mark was everywhere. I could smell him each time I opened the wardrobe. I saw his face by the rowing machine in the garage, looking back at me from behind an upturned bicycle, or standing beside the mower on the lawn. I was used to hearing his bike squeak on the road outside at the end of the day and then the sound of his shoes crunching on the gravel path. I'd pour a glass of water to have it at room temperature so he could drink it when he came in. He was taller than the fence, so I would see him say "Hello" in a silly deep voice as he caught sight of me through the back door. He would be all sweaty and he would sit and talk about his day before he went to shower. In the mornings before he left for work he would bring up my coffee and we would sit and chat, and I would stand up on the bed, usually completely naked, and hug him goodbye. Alix would go to her bedroom window each morning and he would stop the car or his bike on the road outside and wave to her before he moved off.

I would still hear his feet on the gravel, and when I was in the kitchen I would look at the fence and imagine his head moving past. Then I started to see Alix standing by the window upstairs, and that broke me. I thought, *He's never coming home to this house… we need to go.*

It wasn't an easy thing to sell and buy a house all by myself. I'd never done it before. I knew I should pray and try to find out if moving was the right thing to do. I would pray and open my Bible randomly. Each time I kept coming to the story of Lot leaving and Abraham picking up his tent. It felt as if God was telling me, "It's time to move." I decided to test the market and put the house up for sale. I searched around for local estate agents and rang a few to see who could do the best deal. One company offered a good deal and also said they could come round straight away to do a valuation. That afternoon Alix was playing with some friends in the sun room, and when the estate agent walked through, she stopped and peeped at them sitting on the floor. "Oh," she said, "I know those children; they go to my church."

I was surprised and said, "They go to my church too…"

Suddenly it seemed as if the penny had dropped. She put her hand to her mouth and her eyes filled up. "I know who you are," she said.

It felt strange to be a figure people recognized, but she was very kind. As we continued round the house while she took photographs and measurements, she told me she could do an even better deal than the original offer. At the end of the visit she stood in the hallway and said, "If you don't mind, I'm going to commit this sale of the house to prayer." Then she gave me a big hug before walking out to her car. That had certainly never happened to me before! It was Thursday afternoon when she had visited and on Monday she showed a young couple around the house. That evening they made an offer for the full asking price. It was as simple as that.

I'd always thought Hillsborough would be a good place to live. It is a listed Georgian village and I am a history buff, so it was particularly attractive to me. It's also on every main bus route. Dromara was very rural, and with Tori needing to get about and Alix doing ballet, it would make life easier. Before, Mark and I had shared the ferrying, but I was on my own now so I had to be practical. Also it was where Mark's funeral had been held.

We went to view a period town house in the centre of the village. When I walked into the kitchen, my heart leapt. There was a central island with a granite top in the middle, and full-length glass doors looking on to a walled garden. It was the kitchen I had dreamt about all those years earlier, where I'd seen myself chopping vegetables with Tori and another child in the room.

Our offer for the new house had been accepted, and in a

couple of days we would be moving in. I had been to the house several times before the move, and on one visit I sat and prayed in each room. I opened my Bible after I'd prayed and a verse from Ezekiel jumped out at me – chapter 43 and verse 6. It talked about the man standing beside me in the house. I knew the man in the verse referred to God, but for me it was also a sign that God was promising Mark would be beside me too in our new home. Everything had worked so smoothly, I felt that I was in step with God and He was directing my path. There was a sense that this was the right move. But I also knew it was going to be nothing like the move to Dromara, when we had huddled together at the foot of the stairs, all four of us together.

The day of the move, all my old college friends arrived at the house. One of them, Joy, had come with her horsebox, and someone had organized a truck to help keep the costs down. When my former VO, Vince, told the soldiers in the regimental MT (Motor Transport) workshops that I needed help to move, they all said, "We'll do this for Mark." Those boys all arrived at the house really upset, but pleased that they could do one last thing for Mark. I think the removal vehicles caused a bit of a stir with the neighbours, because Hillsborough is quite a posh village. When they saw a battered horsebox attached to a battered old Renault and some truck turn up outside with the furniture, I expect they wondered if the gypsy fair had come to town.

Before anyone packed anything, Valerie walked round the house and took photographs of all the rooms exactly as they were, which she gave me later. Everyone helping had known and cared for Mark just like I did, and they also knew that every little thing in that house was so important to me because at one stage Mark had touched it. I knew I could trust them completely. They told me to get out of the house for a few hours, and I found myself wandering around Lisburn in a complete daze. As I stared in shop windows and sat in a café, my hands clasping a mug of coffee, I kept asking myself, *What has happened to my life?*

The house was practically empty when I returned. I ran my hand along the foot of the stair rail. It was here I used to hide in the cupboard just below and, as Mark was going upstairs, I'd grab his ankle from between the spindles to make him jump. He'd shout out and nearly fall over and I'd be doubled over laughing. It was what I'd always done: I loved jumping out and scaring him and had done it all our married life. In this house I'd sometimes hide in the wardrobe upstairs when I heard him come in. I'd listen to him drop his bags in the hall and put on the TV for the news. He'd call out, "Bren! Brenda! I'm home!" And I would stay quiet, saying nothing and stuffing my fist in my mouth to stop myself laughing. When he came into the bedroom he'd start to open the wardrobe and I'd jump out at him. He'd shout, "Whoa!" and jump back, his arms flying up in the air. He was always so shocked. I got him every time. When I was hiding I'd be thinking, *You're a grown woman, you're forty years old and you're still jumping out on your husband!* It was a happy memory, one to treasure from this home.

As I closed the kitchen door, I had a picture of Tori and me collapsed in laughter in one corner as Mark attempted to pirouette around the room with Alix to help her practise ballet steps. In the bedrooms I remembered his days of painting before we moved in, his back in tatters.

One of the friends told me later that Alix had returned from her school sports day and then spent the last few hours in her empty room, while the furniture was being loaded. They had found her lying on the floor staring up at the ceiling, which her daddy had so lovingly painted "lellow" at her request.

As I walked around it all I tried to feel Mark, but he wasn't there. Then I asked everyone to leave the house because I wanted a few minutes to myself. I went and sat on the living room floor because that was the last room where Mark had been, in his coffin. I started talking to him and I had a chat with God, and then finally I said, "If You would help me now, I still have a chance."

When we arrived at Hillsborough, my teeth were still chattering and I huddled on a chair in the corner of the kitchen while everyone worked around me. Boxes were being carried in and everyone was trying to put the house together in the same way that we had arranged it in Dromara. I watched the army lads carrying in Mark's rowing machine, his weights, and all his army uniforms and mess dress. They took it up to the top floor. Occasionally I suggested places to put cups or bits and pieces, but I felt as if I was watching it all from a great height and this wasn't really my life. It was some sort of dream.

Once everything was in, we all sat down around the kitchen table with a Chinese takeaway and two bottles of gin. We'd told the takeaway we had just moved in and the man at the counter gave us a taster of everything on the menu for £30, which fed us all. The gin and tonic was sloshed into glasses and we all raised our drinks to Mark. Vince, who had been helping all day, finally said, "Mark will be glad that we've taken care of you." I nodded and thanked them all for being there. I was really pleased, grateful, and relieved for their support, but what I really wanted was for them all to go and for me just to be sitting across the table from my Mark.

* * *

We had hardly been in the house a few days when there was a business-like rap at the door. A few seconds later, Tori called up to me from the hall. As I came down the stairs there was a petite lady holding a basket of flowers. She smiled warmly up at me. "Hello, Mrs Hale. I'm Kathryn."

She stepped forward and held the flowers toward me. "I'm from the ladies' branch of the Royal British Legion. We heard you'd moved into the village. I don't want to impose but if you need anything, please ask us because we're here to help. Here's my phone number," she said, placing it on the shelf by the phone. My eyes filled with tears as I took the pretty arrangement, and I could barely speak before she turned and left. I was so moved by the kindness, and that ten months after Mark's death they remembered him and they still cared about us.

CHAPTER 27

December 2010

... a time to plant

Shimmering winter sunshine had turned the lake a deep cobalt blue, and I stopped to pause beside the skeletons of two trees which formed the perfect frame, their spindly branches reflected in the water below. It was Sunday afternoon and a scattering of people were out with dogs and pushchairs, enjoying a rare few hours of December sun. I took a deep breath and continued along the path, so glad that this beautiful park was now almost on our doorstep. I'd needed some air and time to mull things over on my own. Jeffrey Donaldson's visit the day before had left me reeling.

Following that first call a few weeks after the funeral, he'd been a faithful visitor, regularly popping in to say hello and to see how we were getting on. We'd talk about the children, how everything was going for us, and we'd also discuss politics. He had been supportive of my current battle with the MoD over a university bursary for Tori which had been promised by the government for bereaved children. He'd asked me how I would fix things, if

I had a magic wand, and make them better for military families. He really seemed to listen to my ideas and soaked up the stories I was picking up from other families in the same situation. I felt very privileged that he made time to listen, knowing what a busy person he was.

He had phoned ahead the day before, which was unusual. It had been dark by the time he arrived and I had the tea and biscuits ready; I'd noticed he had a sweet tooth. After taking a sip of tea and picking up one of the chocolate biscuits, he looked across at me and said, "Are you still interested in helping out in politics?"

I nodded. "Yes, happy to help in any way I can." I was thinking he must want help with canvassing again as elections would be coming up in the spring, and he would have known I had volunteered with the European elections the year before.

He set his mug down deliberately and then asked, "Would you consider standing for the DUP in the Lagan Valley?"

I wasn't too sure I had heard him right, so I said, "I don't know what you mean." *Surely he can't be asking me to stand for election?* I had no experience; I hadn't even been a local councillor or involved in local politics. A few months earlier I had agreed to be an ambassador for the Army Benevolent Fund, which meant telling our story and appealing for more support around the area, but launching myself into politics was a whole new ball game.

He smiled and said, "You are obviously very political and you are someone who can speak out for the armed forces and their families in Northern Ireland. Would you consider it?"

I went into a sort of dazed state. I was trying to think it over, and as thoughts flashed around my head I felt Mark at my shoulder saying, "Why are you even thinking about this? Say yes!"

I recalled the lines in the poem he had written before he went away:

> *Your lives will continue: and you have much to achieve*
> *I hope you understand and pardon me my leave.*

I thought, *Is this what you were talking about?* If it was, I didn't want to let him down. I was petrified. Eventually I said, "I need to think about it."

He nodded and seemed to expect me to take my time. This was a big decision.

* * *

That morning at church I went for prayer after the service. I said I'd been asked to do something and needed to know whether or not it had come from God, and I explained that it would mean a change of direction in my life. I phoned my minister, Bobby Liddle, when I got home and asked him if we could have a chat about something. He had been very supportive ever since Mark had been killed. When I had moved into the new house he had come and prayed in each room and blessed the house, asking for God's peace to be with us there. I hoped talking with him would help me as I considered Jeffrey's proposal.

Why me, Lord? I said silently, half to myself and half in prayer. A Lycra-clad runner jogged past me on the path and I watched a woman with a beanie hat throwing a ball for her Labrador across the closely cropped grass.

My life had been turned upside down in the last eighteen months. In November I'd attended a dinner in London where I had been presented with the Elizabeth Cross. This is the emblem given to the next of kin of British service personnel killed in action. I didn't want the medal, I'd told the Commanding Officer, Rob Thomson, quite plainly. He'd said it had to be presented properly and I said, "No, no, you just give it to me if you want." Rob told me it was usually the Lord Lieutenant who made the presentation, but I said he needed to understand that neither Mark nor I had gone to our degree ceremonies as we didn't like that kind of thing. We didn't want the fuss.

Eventually I had agreed to go to a small dinner he was organizing with members of the Officers' Mess in Mayfair, to which the father of Paul Mervis was also invited. Rob took me aside and made a quiet presentation in a side room. I suppose I hadn't wanted to receive it because it was another sign that Mark was never coming home. When the regiment had been returning last year part of me expected him to walk in through the door or turn up at the Mess during the lunch. I still couldn't believe he had been taken from us forever.

That night after the dinner was when it came home to me how alone I was. Mark had always protected me; he'd had my back. Now I was truly alone and I had begun to doubt my judgment. I wasn't even sure I could trust some of those who said they were supporting me. *Perhaps standing for election would be the focus I needed to stop me dwelling on that terrible loneliness?*

As I thought again about Jeffrey's invitation, I began to see why he might want me to stand. They were changing the boundary in the Lagan Valley and there was a chance of the DUP getting a fourth seat. The party were expanding and looking to modernize and build their voter base as well. Perhaps they thought a soldier's wife might appeal to more voters. The words from Mark's verse kept coming back to me: "you have much to achieve". *Did he know? Had he seen something? Or was he given a sign that there was something else for me?*

Although I loved talking politics, the whole idea of standing for election was terrifying. Having my face on a poster went against everything I knew, after living quietly for years and keeping my head below the parapet because of Mark's job. I had felt physically sick the previous evening when I'd thought about my photograph being plastered on lampposts. I suppose I'd been a very private person with a tight-knit group of friends; I wasn't known in the area. But Mark's death had changed that.

I turned to stare out across the lake where a flock of geese were swooping down to land. They stretched out their wings and arched their necks, water spraying up from their webbed feet like expert water skiers. There was a chilly nip in the air and the sun was beginning to sink into the trees on the far bank. I turned back on myself and headed along the path the way I'd come. *What do you want, Brenda?* I mulled that question over in my head. Although I was a private person, I knew I wasn't afraid to speak out. There were times when no one could stop me.

The previous summer we had visited Mark's former boss who had served with him in Afghanistan. Lt Col Darren Denning and his family had made us so welcome at their home in Virginia, where they were currently posted. During the trip we had spent a few days in Washington, visiting Alexandria en route. One morning the girls and I were walking down a street enjoying the shops and the scenery, when I overheard what two American women walking in front of us were saying in very loud voices. They were being very critical about British soldiers for some reason and saying how glad they were that their husbands weren't serving with any British regiments. I must have looked daggers because Tori shook her head. "Don't say anything, Mum. Walk past," she'd hissed.

We quickly overtook them, but after we'd gone a few steps I couldn't resist turning around and facing them both. I said, "You should really keep your voices down. Your opinions are wrong. My husband served with the British army in an American war in the Middle East and died for it. And by the way, our army is the best in the world. Perhaps another time you'll be more aware of who is walking behind you in the streets."

They looked shocked as I turned on my heels and walked on. There was no way I could let them get away with saying that kind of thing. Mark had been right to warn people about his "fiery" wife. I was passionate about tackling injustice; perhaps standing for election was a way to put that into action. *Could I be a voice for others who aren't able to speak up? You know what,* I thought, *I have to be selected by the party, and I might not even be selected.* In fact, the chances of being selected and then being elected seemed pretty slim. *Maybe giving it a go isn't such a risk.*

* * *

Bobby arrived in time for a cup of tea the following afternoon, and as we sat at the table I began to explain about Jeffrey's visit. He seemed surprised when I told him, but his face was a picture of calm, as ever. It was a few moments before he spoke. "There's a number of things you may want to think about, Brenda. One is the impact on Tori and Alix, because they are your top priority at the moment, and the highly erratic nature of being in politics is likely to impact on them."

I turned the mug around in my hands. I knew he was right.

Then he gave me a grim smile and said, "Of course, you'd be going into the 'bear pit', because that's what politics is… You need to think about whether you can cope with that. It's a tough environment." He asked me a bit about my view of politics and I explained about my interest from a young age and how my degree had fuelled that passion. When I'd finished speaking, he pushed his chair back from the table and looked directly at me. "The thing is, Brenda, when the Lord closes one door He very often opens another one. Sometimes He uses things we've been on the periphery of before to open doors for us. This may be a way the Lord is wanting to use you, and it isn't directly involved with your life with Mark. This is now about Brenda Hale."

We talked about the impact the job could have on my spiritual life and how committed I was to the DUP. I asked if it would help for him to talk with Jeffrey, and he said he would speak with him. He was concerned about how I would survive as a single mum with two girls, trying to keep life and limb together, mentally and physically. Before he left, he prayed with me about the decision I had to make. Standing by the door, he smiled and said, "You should know, if it all goes ahead, I will not be a member of the DUP and I won't be knocking on doors on your behalf, but I will be supportive of you in politics. Of course, you won't know if this is the way the Lord is leading you unless you push the door."

Standing looking out at the fading afternoon light on the garden wall, I felt strangely peaceful. Bobby had raised some important issues, but he hadn't discouraged me. In fact, he had encouraged me to "push the door".

A few days later I picked up the phone and told Jeffrey I would like to go ahead. *Quite likely it will all come to nothing in the end,* I thought.

May 2011

My feet were sore and I was so tired of talking to complete strangers. It had been the final day of door knocking, visits, and media interviews during what had begun to feel like a six-week marathon. I sank down on the settee and slid off my shoes, closing my eyes. *If Mark were here he would make me a hot drink now and tell me to put my feet up.* I missed that tap on the shoulder and his voice saying, "Sweetie, do you want a cup of tea?"

Alix was asleep and Tori was in the bath. They had both done so well, trailing round the streets with me these last few weeks of canvassing. Whether it was stuffing envelopes or photocopying fliers, Alix had willingly lent a hand. When the campaign posters had first gone up she had enjoyed spotting them as we drove about, but a couple of days earlier when I picked her up from school, she said, "Oh, Mummy, there's another one of your posters. When can we take them down again?" It can't have been easy seeing my face everywhere and having her friends at school make comments. Tori had done her bit too, keeping things going at home, making tea and putting on washing, even though she was now heading into serious revision for her A Level exams. Both the girls had supported my campaign wholeheartedly. I couldn't have wished for anything more… except for their daddy to be there.

Mark knew I loved politics, and studying subjects like housing, policing, and criminology as part of my degree had fuelled that passion. No matter where we moved to, I always registered to vote. We would go to the voting booths and I would tell Mark what each candidate was standing for and their policies, even what was behind the spin in their campaign speak. Politically he trusted me one hundred per cent. I always took an interest in international politics, and I particularly watched American foreign policy because I believed it had a direct effect on our foreign policy and how that would affect us as a British army family.

I didn't know if I'd done enough to convince those undecided voters, but in a few days we'd know more. The following day was polling day and Tori would be casting her first vote, hopefully with a tick against my name! The whole thing was still very unreal and seemed to have a momentum of its own.

Since I'd agreed to stand, everything had moved rapidly. The selection had gone through smoothly and now here I was, canvassing votes in the hope of being elected as an assembly member for Lagan Valley.

That weekend we would also be celebrating Tori's eighteenth birthday. I'd booked a private dining room at the Merchant Hotel in Belfast. There would be eighteen of us – close family and a few of Tori's friends. I'd given her the choice to have a car or a meal at a five-star hotel. She'd gone for the meal at the hotel. It would be an occasion to remember, although not without tears. We'd all be aware of that empty chair at the table.

I reached for my laptop and flicked through some emails. I still half expected to see one from Mark, asking me about the girls. Sometimes losing him would hit me like a wave, knocking me off my feet. Each time I struggled to get back up.

* * *

I turned the cardboard cup around in my hands nervously. The tension was really starting to ratchet up. Today was Saturday, the second day of counting, and according to Northern Ireland's proportional representation system, the votes were gradually being redistributed back to other candidates as the ones with the fewest votes were knocked out. It was a tense and drawn-out process, which I was only just coming to grips with. My DUP colleagues were assuring me I had nothing to worry about and that my initial vote tally meant I was most likely to get through. But I didn't like to take anything for granted.

Down in the gym of Lisburn Leisureplex, the next round of counting had started in earnest. Earlier we'd all celebrated when another party member had their seat confirmed. I looked around the café, which was filled with smartly dressed groups of people poring over phones and laptops, or clasping clipboards and shuffling bundles of papers. Tori was sitting opposite, playing on her phone, and Alix was queuing at the café bar for food. I knew I'd be incredibly disappointed if I didn't win, but there would also be a certain amount of relief. Being elected was, quite frankly, terrifying me at that moment.

Tori looked up and grinned. "I hope you get in soon, Mum, or we're hardly going to have time to change for tonight!"

"I know, honey… I'm sorry you've both been stuck here all day."

Alix returned with some sandwiches and an iced bun, which she plonked in the middle of the table. "I bought enough for everyone," she said.

Tori picked up one of the packets of sandwiches and examined it.

I smiled and said, "You carry on, Alix. I can't eat a thing at the moment."

It was true: I had no appetite at all. But that was nothing new. Since Mark's death I hadn't wanted to eat. I forced myself to occasionally, but I'd lost a stone and a half in the first few months. Food still didn't interest me. I lived on coffee.

* * *

It was about half past three when they finally called everyone back down again. I stood beside other party members and fellow candidates, and with Tori and Alix either side of me on the bright blue gym floor. Long tables were arranged in an open-ended rectangle in the centre, where dozens of people sat behind papers and ballot boxes. As the official stepped toward the microphone to announce the results of the latest count, I felt a knot clench in my stomach. In a moment I'd know whether all the hard work had paid off.

There had been so much to come to grips with during the past few months. I'd met with the DUP team, studied the party manifesto, and begun to make myself aware of how to answer key questions on issues like education, health, and housing, until I felt my brain was boiled with information. The party were very supportive about my fight for a better deal for the military and their families. They knew that Northern Ireland made up three per cent of the UK population and yet supplied four per cent of the UK armed forces and an incredible twenty per cent of its reserve forces. I was standing for a party in a part of the UK that supplied more of its men and women to the armed forces than any other. I knew my story resounded with so many people. The previous day one of the other candidates had asked me if I was nervous about going home and not knowing whether I was elected or not. I said, "No, nerves to me is waiting on a phone call when you know your husband is walking down Pharmacy Road." That was the main road in Afghanistan. I had no reason to be worried compared to the fear that Mark and his soldiers had walked with every day of that operation, and no result today could be as life changing as the news I had received on 13 August 2009.

The announcer's words floated over my head as I heard my name being read out as the successful DUP candidate for Lagan Valley. People were shaking my hand and giving me hugs, while Tori and Alix were jumping about next to me. Despite what everyone had been telling me, I was shocked. All I could think was, *How did that happen?*

The next hour or so was a blur. I heard that the First Minister and party leader Peter Robinson was coming across to congratulate us as we had gained an extra seat in Lagan Valley, moving the DUP members up from three to four. I remember seeing Jeffrey beaming at me, and I hugged both the girls before being led to the microphone to try to say something coherent. I was choking back tears as I spoke. "I know my husband Mark would have been proud of me today. He always knew I had a voice. He used to have to listen to it! Mark is my ultimate inspiration. He served his country with total conviction and he laid down his life on behalf of others…"

I thanked God, the girls, my family and friends, and members of the party, especially Jeffrey, for their support. Then I said, "I have a voice here and I am going to use it to secure more rights for women who have suffered a similar ordeal. I was a military wife for twenty-two years and I feel that I have a responsibility to speak out on behalf of military wives who are much younger and who have no platform to fight for what they need. Army wives are a very special breed of person. We are strong and we are tough, and we have to use that toughness and just keep moving forward."

* * *

A few hours later, at Tori's birthday celebration, the flames on the candles were flickering, scattering golden drops of light on the silver stands and cutlery around the table. The room was dimly lit with soft wall lamps, and the rich coloured carpet and classic wallpaper wrapped around us, providing a luxurious sense of occasion. I picked up the crisp linen napkin and enjoyed the touch of the damask tablecloth against my hand. All around were our nearest and dearest. The lads were in DJs or suits; the girls all carefully made up and dressed in their finery. Tori looked particularly stunning in a short black and white cocktail dress and high heels. *How have eighteen years passed since Mark was sitting beside me in the hospital bed with her in his arms?* His absence was a physical pain that made me catch my breath.

Local photographer Brian Thompson was treating Tori like a celebrity as he captured every part of the occasion on camera, from the first arrivals to toasts at the table. He later told me his time was a gift for Tori, and said, "I have two daughters, and God willing I'll be there for their eighteenth birthdays." As the meal progressed, we all sang "Happy birthday", and Tori amazed me by standing up to make a toast.

Gripping the edge of the table, she looked across at me and then smiled around at everyone. I couldn't believe she could keep her voice steady as she said, "I want to make a toast to my dad.

The person I am today is because of my mum and dad." She said how much she loved her dad and how proud she was of me for being strong and for standing for election and getting through. Tears were streaming down my face by the time we stood to raise our glasses, and I could see my sister and auntie and uncle were also struggling to control their emotions. I sipped the champagne slowly, trying to smile and take it all in. My Auntie Anne patted my hand gently, and I looked across at Tori and Alix. I was staring down the tunnel of time, seeing the weddings and the grandchildren coming. I was going to miss sharing all that with the man who loved these girls as much as I did. *You should be here tonight, Mark, and one day it should be you walking her down the aisle.* I wanted to celebrate, but inside I was mourning that loss for my children.

Chapter 28

May 2011

... a time to start

Standing in the doorway, I took in the wide, dark-wood desk with the phone and the wire in-tray, the empty bookshelves, and a bundle of papers waiting to be looked through on the shelf at the side. I had a lot of reading to do and a lot to learn. From here it looked like a mountain to climb. As I wandered round the room and set my bag down on a chair, I still couldn't believe this was to be my office for the next five years. My PA Nicola said she would pop down and fetch us a coffee, and suddenly I was alone. I sank down into the chair and picked up the phone, then put it down again and started to giggle. *If you could see me now, Mark!*

On that Monday after the count I trooped into Stormont with the rest of the newly elected members. It felt like the first day at a new school. We all had to sign our names at a table on the floor of the chamber. As I walked into the cavernous room with its deep blue carpet, the tiers of benches and blue padded seating set against wood-panelled walls with the public gallery above, I was overwhelmed by the gravity of what we were about to do. I was becoming a part of the history that had been made in this building, and a part of the new devolved government of a peaceful Northern Ireland.

The last time I had been in this building was when I was thirteen and I'd come on a visit with the church youth group. We'd sat in the public gallery and looked down on the debates. I was fascinated by politics even at that age. A lot had changed since, but my sense of awe at being elected to be a part of this democratic process was even greater.

I swivelled round in my chair, realizing that for the first time since I was sixteen years old I was doing something on my own that Mark didn't have any part in. And yet he did. He was the reason I was sitting here. He was my inspiration for the job. Mark loved his boys and he was proud of their courage, many of them just eighteen or nineteen years old. They were terrified, sometimes crying with fear every time they had to put on body armour and boots, not knowing if their next step was going to blow them to kingdom come. Mark didn't have to go out on patrol; he went the extra mile because the boys needed to be "trimmed" when they came back in. He put himself literally on the line and he gave absolutely everything. He did the final thing for his boys. He didn't call for help; he was the help. I thought of the verses in Isaiah when God said, *Whom shall I send?* Maybe God was telling Mark that those boys needed help, and God sent him.

I gulped back a sob. *No good crying on the job, Mrs Hale,* I thought, just as the door swung open and Nicola carried in two steaming mugs of coffee. She pushed one across to me, then drew up a chair and smiled. "Have you got time for us to go through some of these papers?" she asked, nodding to the pile on one corner of the desk.

Several hours later I was about to leave for the day, but instead of going toward the stairs I headed to the front of the building and into the members' bar. As I nudged open the door there were a few people drinking at the bar, but I walked toward one of the long windows which looked down on the stretch of drive with its regal avenue of trees and lampposts leading to the Edward Carson statue. It was that special time of early evening when a golden light was falling through the trees, bathing the grass and the stonework with a hazy glow and lighting up the edges of the figure's outstretched arm. Here I was, standing on the brink of a new adventure.

I looked down at the pathway laid out before me and I couldn't see where it would end; it disappeared into the haze of the sun. I breathed in that view and prayed that God would help me to be His voice and His hands and feet here in Stormont. I had a list of reasons why I shouldn't be there. I was shy. I hated walking into a room full of strangers. I didn't enjoy having to network. I wasn't good at thinking on my feet. I was really good at one-liners, but I put my foot in it all the time. And I was still deeply in mourning for a man I'd been in love with for twenty-four years.

I didn't know if I would ever finish grieving. But Mark was my inspiration every day. All the love I still had for him I would channel into fighting injustice and making sure our forces' families were heard and treated fairly. *I'll never forget that I married a soldier, because I am still that soldier's wife.*

September 2016

... a time to reflect

The Speaker calls, "Order, order," and I look around the chamber. Some faces have changed but most of us have returned for another term. At my second election in May 2016, I was voted in for another five years. Looking back, I can see my life has been divided into two distinct chapters: the young girl who married a soldier would never have believed where the widow stands today. I see myself as a shadow, but others see substance and a force to be reckoned with. My life has changed since Mark's death, from just existing in the beginning to campaigning for a cause we both believe in.

After my meeting with Bob Ainsworth in Whitehall, my life began to move at a pace that was so fast I just couldn't catch up with myself, as we say in Northern Ireland. One of Mark's close army friends, Carl "Chuckles" Boswell, wanted to raise some significant money for the charity that was helping me, so he and a few of Mark's other friends, including Will Wells, P. J. Luard, and Nigel Moreland, planned to run from John O' Groats to

Land's End – 851 miles over seventeen days, which would involve running a double marathon each day. They completed the run on 26 June – Armed Forces Day – and raised funds for the Army Benevolent Fund, the Rifles Association, and Help for Heroes. It was called the "Undentable Run" in memory of Mark, and I know he would have been impressed with their achievement.

I joined in supporting them on the route, as did TV crews, other army mates, and some big names. Along the way I met the families of soldiers who had returned with life-changing injuries, and other bereaved families of those who had sadly followed Mark through Wootton Bassett. They all had the same story to tell. They told me how they had had to fight for every piece of help they received. It was emotionally exhausting listening to their battles because their fight should have ended in Afghanistan. The common thread in all my meetings and conversations was that they were being let down by the system they had fought to protect.

I felt burdened by what I heard. For Mark, it was always about "the blokes", and it was for his blokes he died, and so for me, my love for him was transferred to "the blokes", and I was filled with a sense of purpose that in the absence of the government honouring him and his boys, I would. But I didn't know where to begin.

That same year, in May 2010, the Army Benevolent Fund – which we know as "The Soldiers' Charity" – approached me and asked me to be one of their ambassadors. I was so humbled and pleased to be given the opportunity to be able to give something back. Through my role I began to meet service personnel of all cap badges and numerous operations, men and women who willingly took their country's shilling and served at home and abroad. Sadly, the stories they so generously shared with me would often end the same way, with difficulties in accessing services and advice, and no one seemed to listen. My blood boiled, and the fire that Mark had seen in me I now saw in myself. I knew something had to be done and someone had to do it, but who? I thought I was too tired, too much in pain, and too shy to do anything but help from the sidelines.

As 2011 dawned, Jeffrey Donaldson continued to pop in every few weeks just to check if I was making headway with the MoD, as my next battle was to secure Tori's university bursary for bereaved children. There had been a government headline claiming they would support them, but when I pursued it I was told by Downing Street it was only an aspiration. I was furious. Tori was waiting for her A Level results and universities were sending offers, but without this bursary there was no way I, as a widow, could afford this next step in her education. I discussed this with Jeffrey and he said he would raise it with the Prime Minister on the floor of the House, but advised me to write to him directly and to bluntly state my case. I did.

As I wrote, I prayed my pen would be my sword. The two-pronged approach worked, and Tori was one of the first recipients of the university bursary. Since my battle, the government now supports all children bereaved since 2001 with a university bursary. My first election success was made sweeter with the knowledge that children like Tori were being helped to become productive adults who would eventually be able to pay back into the system.

That battle was won, but not yet the war. There were so many issues, and the troubled history of Northern Ireland made for many complex layers that acted like a "Berlin Wall", preventing service families and veterans accessing help when they needed it. And so began the toing and froing to meetings with Whitehall officials, including meetings with David Cameron at Westminster. The battle for the Military Covenant is not a constituency one, and so I had to self-finance the flights and hotels for these meetings, but it was worth every penny of Mark's pension.

Sitting before officials and going over and over the details of Mark's death and the consequent failures in the system was traumatizing and difficult. My teeth would begin to chatter again and it would take weeks to recalibrate myself after each meeting. I would then have to steel myself and gather strength to push for yet another meeting. I didn't give up. I continued to meet many ex-forces groups. There were so many charities and we were all calling for the same thing. We were simply asking to be listened to, to be looked after, to be given a hand up, not a handout.

One of the markers I look back on was in 2013, as St Patrick's Day approached. I was invited to visit Washington as a member of the Office of First Minister and Deputy First Minister Committee. In between official meetings I would be able to use my spare time to try to make contacts with the Senate and US military charities. I knew the Americans had the GI Bill and I was keen to see how that was implemented and how the government worked with military charities, in comparison to how it was done in the UK.

The Northern Ireland Office in Washington set up meetings for me with a senior military aide in the British Embassy, with whom I was to meet shortly after landing. A taxi dropped me outside the building and I said a quick prayer as I wondered how on earth an army wife had ended up there. I took some courage that my first contact was Lt Col Ash Alexander Cooper, an army friend who had served with Mark in Afghanistan, so at least I had a familiar face close by.

I had nothing to worry about. The meeting went well and was an eye-opener for the British army colonel Fred Hargreaves, who immediately organized an informal meeting for me in the White House two days later. Again my teeth began to chatter. I was petrified, but somehow I always seemed to be in the right place at the right time.

Over the next few days I could hardly believe what was happening to me. The President was hosting a lunch for a handful of politicians from Northern Ireland and the Republic of Ireland to mark St Patrick's Day, and there I was at the table next to President Obama. As I chatted to the Californian Senator seated to my left, my story spilled out. I watched as his eyes filled with tears and he told me of his military service and a little of how the US system works. The US forces have Gold Star and Blue Star families. The Gold Star families are those who are bereaved, and the name describes how they try to look after them.

I returned from Washington drained but more determined than ever that our armed forces should be treated with decency and respect, and that the UK government should find ways to say "Yes" to their requests instead of trying to justify why they are saying "No".

No system is perfect – we shouldn't expect it to be – but we do expect a system that cares and that works.

* * *

Back in the chamber at Stormont, I would breathe in deeply and in my mind reach out for Mark. The IED that killed him in 2009 had been laid by a particularly lethal Taliban cell. I now knew that Lt Col Ash Alexander-Cooper had been part of one of the last missions of his tour that same year which captured the ringleader of the cell. They mounted a crossing of the Helmand River late one night and swam into the enemy safe haven to lie in wait for him. When they captured him, he went to court and was jailed for life.

Time has moved on but hearts stand still. It gets easier to hide the pain and hurt of losing him, missing him, and wanting him, but it never subsides, never ebbs. It always flows. I close my eyes and look for his smile, then inhale deeply, trying to smell his aftershave, feeling that stab of loneliness again. The fight goes on, and after speaking with the Defence Select Committee on a cold, dark November evening in Belfast, I am to meet them in 2017 to press for an inquiry into how bereaved families are treated and how bereaved children are looked after. I know it's not a magic wand, but if the decision makers are actively listening, that is a step in the right direction.

The unsettled waters of Northern Irish politics and the uneasy mandatory coalition between two parties with polarised ideologies always meant that compromise was a better but bitter pill to swallow. Having lost my seat in the snap election of March 2017, and with the likelihood of a further Stormont election, I wait to see what God has planned for me. My lobbying for Armed Forces issues will continue as I have been appointed to the Covenant Forces Reference Group in Westminster as the voice for Northern Ireland and I will continue to serve those that have served us.

The last seven years have been hectic, blurred, and often frantic. We Hale girls have spent every significant date travelling around the world visiting our army friends. To be honest, it has been my way of coping with the pain, by running away. But I've come to realize that the pain travels with you: it sneaks into the suitcase, or between the pages of the passport. Every country stamped is a country without Mark. I look back on French summers spent with the Thomson family as the only place where I could really breathe. Among the hustle, bustle, and gentle family chaos that Alix could get lost in and where I could hide, I knew nothing needed to be explained or spoken. I am so grateful to the many who have supported me in the past few years, including the Moreland brothers for just letting me be me, and the Hills for always being there, especially in the immediate hours after Mark was killed. And Footy (Sox), who was there from the beginning. We are blessed.

Our army friends and church family have been our lifesavers in a world that was completely strange to us, following that forcible ejection from all we ever knew into what we call "Civvy Street". It is a different world with a different language and with new rules and paths to negotiate, but we have managed, thanks to our very close network of friends. My church at Legacurry has been a place of love and rest, where the congregation have taken ownership of us and shielded us. The solid teaching of Bobby and the pastoral care of the church elders have been lights in the darkest days, a safe place to rant at God and demand that He justify His actions, before I realize with quiet acceptance that He is God. Mark was right: I need to be still and listen.

I cast my mind back to Tori's first day at university, when all the dads were helping their daughters settle into halls of residence and we Hales did it as best we could. At her graduation, when she wore her dad's medals so proudly, I wanted to share the moment and silently whispered to Mark, "How clever we are to have a girl like Tori. Didn't we do well?" When Alix takes her sailing dinghy out on the sea and I can see her skimming across the waves, I can feel Mark's grin spreading across his face as he watches his baby girl joining in the Strangford Regatta. He would be so proud of what our girls have achieved and where we are now, and we have done it all for him, living as honourably as we can in his memory.

I am often asked to speak at military and church events about our journey and faith. It never gets easier, but I am pleased that Mark's life and his faith are reflected in us, and it's on his example we have based our lives. It may seem that we idolize him, and we do, but only as a gift from God. Knowing the outcome, I would do it all again, for not to have shared his life would have been much worse. The minute he crossed my path something inside me knew. I know God was very firmly in control, and I give thanks for that. I thank God for our old friends and the new friends He has sent to enrich our lives and share our journey, however long that might be. Our time is in His hands.

Semper Fidelis... this one's for you xx